Strategies for the Threshold #10

Dealing with Lilith:
Spirit of Dispossession

Anne Hamilton

Dealing with Lilith: Spirit of Dispossession

Strategies for the Threshold #10

© Anne Hamilton 2024

Published by Armour Books
P. O. Box 492, Corinda QLD 4075 Australia

Cover images: Kevin Carden 'A woman's mind is open to see a fierce battle' | Lightstock; iloveotto 'Asia style textures and backgrounds' | canstockphoto.com; Diego Passadori 'Brown wooden surface' | Unsplash.com

Interior Design and Typeset by Beckon Creative

ISBN: 978-1-925380-74-3

 A catalogue record for this book is available from the National Library of Australia

All rights reserved. No part of this publication may be reproduced, stored in, or introduced into a retrieval system, or transmitted, in any form, or by any means (electronic, mechanical, photocopying, recording or otherwise) without the prior written permission of the publisher.

Note: Australian spelling and grammar conventions are used throughout this book.

Strategies for the Threshold #10

Dealing with Lilith:
Spirit of Dispossession

Anne Hamilton

Scripture quotations marked ASV are taken from the American Standard Version of the Bible. Public domain.

Scripture quotations marked BLB are taken from the The Blue Letter Bible. Used by permission. blueletterbible.org

Scripture quotations marked BSB are taken from the The Holy Bible, Berean Study Bible, BSB Copyright ©2016 by Bible Hub Used by Permission. All Rights Reserved Worldwide.

Scripture quotations marked CSB are taken The Christian Standard Bible. Copyright © 2017 by Holman Bible Publishers. Used by permission. Christian Standard Bible®, and CSB® are federally registered trademarks of Holman Bible Publishers, all rights reserved.

Scripture quotations marked ESV are taken from the ESV® Bible (The Holy Bible, English Standard Version®), copyright © 2001 by Crossway, a publishing ministry of Good News Publishers. Used by permission. All rights reserved.

Scripture quotations marked GNT are from the Good News Translation in Today's English Version—Second Edition Copyright © 1992 by American Bible Society. Used by Permission.

Scripture quotations marked ISV are taken from the Holy Bible: International Standard Version®. Copyright © 1996-forever by The ISV Foundation. ALL RIGHTS RESERVED INTERNATIONALLY. Used by permission.

Scripture quotations marked NASB are taken from the New American Standard Bible®, Copyright © 1960, 1962, 1963, 1968, 1971, 1972, 1973, 1975, 1977, 1995 by The Lockman Foundation. Used by permission. (www.Lockman.org)

Scripture quotations marked NIV are taken from the Holy Bible, New International Version®, NIV®. Copyright © 1973, 1978, 1984, 2011 by Biblica, Inc.™ Used by permission of Zondervan. All rights reserved worldwide. www.zondervan.com The "NIV" and "New International Version" are trademarks registered in the United States Patent and Trademark Office by Biblica, Inc.™.

Scripture quotations marked NKJV are taken from the New King James Version. Copyright © 1982 by Thomas Nelson, Inc. Used by permission. All rights reserved.

Scripture quotations marked NLT are taken from the Holy Bible, New Living Translation, copyright 1996, 2004. Used by permission of Tyndale House Publishers, Inc., Wheaton, Illinois 60189. All rights reserved.

Scripture quotations marked WEB are taken from the World English Bible, a modernisation of the American Standard Version (ASV). Public domain.

Other Books By Anne Hamilton

Jesus and the Healing of History Series

1 *Like Wildflowers, Suddenly*
2 *Bent World, Bright Wings*
3 *Silk Shadows, Rings of Gold*
4 *Where His Feet Pass*
5 *The Singing Silence*
6 *In the Meshes of the Net*
7 *Interpreted by Love*

Devotional Theology series

God's Poetry: The Identity & Destiny Encoded in Your Name
God's Panoply: The Armour of God & the Kiss of Heaven
God's Pageantry: The Threshold Guardians & the Covenant Defender
God's Pottery: The Sea of Names & the Pierced Inheritance
God's Priority: World-Mending & Generational Testing
More Precious than Pearls (with *Natalie Tensen*)
As Resplendent As Rubies (with *Natalie Tensen*)
As Exceptional as Sapphires (with *Donna Ho*)
Spiritual Legal Rights (with *Janice Sergison*)
Spiritual Legal Rights II (with *Janice Sergison*)

Mystery, Majesty and Mathematics in John's Gospel

The Elijah Tapestry: John 1 and 21
The Summoning of Time: John 2 and 20

Thank you

Joy	Jess	Sean
Richard	Kevin	Joan
Janice	Judy	Max
Julie	Michelle	Mary
Jill	Ruth	Mark
Jenny	Therese	Kathy
Jenny	Sharon	Lucy
Jenny	Michael	Eugene
Bryce	Susan	Beck

Contents

Introduction		9
Prayer before starting		13
1	**Appointment and Disappointment**	15
	Prayer	45
2	**Weaving History and Scripture**	47
	Prayer	151
3	**Just Ask Me**	157
	Prayer for *Doing*	192
	Prayer for *Being*	193
4	**Armament for Battle**	197
	Prayer	219
5	**Threshing Floors**	223
	Prayer	249
6	**Jesus, Just Jesus**	251
	Prayer	268
Appendix 1	Summary of Lilith's Tactics	271
Appendix 2	Summary	275
Endnotes		281

Introduction

I WAS INCREDIBLY NAÏVE when I began to write this book. I thought that Lilith, the vampire spirit, was easy to overcome. I'd encountered her once when she'd raged at me after a prayer ministry session. I'd bundled her into the mix with the spirit of abuse at the very last moment, dismissing them both as a duo. She turned up later, livid and violently threatening.

After a moment of shock and surprise, I'd simply said, 'I'm not discussing this. If you have any problems with what I did, you take it up directly with Jesus of Nazareth.' And that was that. She was gone.

So, I thought as I started this book, *Lilith? No worries, not a problem*.

Fortunately, about halfway through the book, I took off the month of November—this was 2022—for my annual adventure into John's gospel. Each year, I spend time investigating the numeric and lyric structure of John's dazzling poem, matching up verses at the beginning and the end. His gospel is an epic in the Hebrew style, full of symmetrical mirroring. Sometimes the parallelisms are incredibly easy to see, and sometimes they're such a serious intellectual challenge my brain hurts.

The reason I follow this method of analysis is because it unearths beautiful elements in the text that are generally overlooked. The only time I'd heard of the fearsome Canaanite goddess Anat before I found allusions to her in the second and second-last chapters of John's gospel was when I was analysing the name exchange between Joseph and Pharaoh in *Name Covenant: Invitation to Friendship*. But I hadn't looked at Anat's story back then because it didn't seem relevant. But now, as a profile of her began to emerge, I realised she was another face of Lilith. More importantly and unexpectedly, she was a major opponent of Jesus.

As a picture of her built up, I also began to recognise her presence during prayer ministry. That's when I realised how naïve I was to think she's easy to remove. Usually when it comes to threshold spirits, people want them gone *now*. Or preferably, *yesterday*. But to my enormous surprise, they often hesitate over Anat. *What kind of hook does she have*, I wondered, *that our first reaction is to placate her?* Once I began to understand that, I realised I'd have to start this book over.

It's already overlong, so I've entirely left out stories I'd like to have included, particularly Phinehas' covenant of peace and the episode involving Caleb's daughter Achsah. There's so much more.

Regarding terminology: when I use the name 'Lilith', I'm referring to this spirit in her vampire aspect—as one who drains life, sucks us dry, leaves us hollow. When I use the name 'Anat', I'm referring her warmonger aspect—as one who dispossesses and disinherits us. Sometimes I may even seem to use the names interchangeably, but I've intentionally tried to distinguish between their different operational characters.

In the mid-nineteenth century, Éliphas Lévi, the occultist responsible for promoting the pentagram as a symbol of witchcraft—thus overturning its millennia-long association with Trinity, resurrection and love—created a symbol known as the Sigil of Baphomet. It features an inverted pentagram, an image of a goat's head, the name of Leviathan in Hebrew and the names, Samael and Lilith, in English. And a century ago, the Irish writer James Joyce called Lilith the 'patron of abortions' in *Ulysses*.

Since then, Lilith has become far more common in literature and gaming, and emerged as a feminist icon. Anat on the other hand has remained obscure. Yet she's of tremendous significance in the life of Jesus. His campaign against her never let up. From His very first miracle at the wedding in Cana to that wondrous moment when He revealed Himself in the garden after the resurrection, He took ground against Anat. On many occasions He was at war with different spirits but His opening and closing salvos were against Anat and her allies.

A virtually unknown goddess featuring so prominently in Scripture while totally escaping our notice may seem impossible. But that's part of Anat's special genius—she's mastered the strategic art of being underrated and underestimated.

Quite likely, you've never heard of her before. I'd certainly overlooked her until I came across her 'by chance' while looking through a list of Hebrew words for *appointed time*. In fact, that's another weapon in her arsenal—she claims to be in charge of *appointed time* and thus to govern our fate.

The problem is—too many of us believe her. By and large, the prophets did. That's a seriously unpleasant thought. Yet I believe it's the reason why God has been so slow in revealing how to deal with this spirit of dispossession. So I wouldn't make the same mistakes they did. Or pass them on to you.

Anne
March 2024

Prayer

before starting

Gracious Lord of lights and love, I put all appointed times before You, including the appointed time for reading this book. I ask that You sanctify the time—sanctify my mornings and evenings, sanctify the day and the night, sanctify my space of learning as I set myself to face the issues that have taken me away from You.

Dwell in me, Lord, and cause me to dwell in You.

En*courage* me, give me the courage to face my fears and to walk hand-in-hand with Jesus of Nazareth, Your beloved Son, into the terrifying glory of the Fear of the Lord. Grant me the strength to keep going, to persevere, to be ever more faithful to You, to uplift Your name and to take up my calling as You direct.

Kiss me with Your armour and gird me with the Fruit of Your Spirit in full, ripe measure. Hide me under the shadow of Your prayer shawl, even in the fiercest battle.

In the name of Jesus of Nazareth.

Amen.

1
Appointment and Disappointment

WHEN THE HEAD OF OUR DEPARTMENT was about to retire, two of my colleagues put their hands up for promotion. Their rivalry was so friendly that they helped each other in filling out the application forms. The rest of the department found it difficult to choose which one of them to back—because, actually, their talents complemented each other brilliantly. So we encouraged them both, recalling stories that showcased their different abilities as well as suggesting ways their applications could be bettered.

In the end, after a drawn-out process of multiple interviews before a selection panel, neither of them was promoted. The position went to a complete outsider. My colleagues were given a confusing explanation: on the one hand, they were told they were too old—because they were in their mid-forties, they were allegedly lacking in innovative ideas. On the other hand, they were too young—because if either of them got the position, then they'd likely hold it for the best part of twenty years, thus creating a stranglehold on a prized and coveted appointment.

The actual appointee, the complete outsider, was in his early twenties. Not only was he totally inexperienced in leadership, he knew nothing—literally *nothing*—about our department's speciality, our processes, or the operational procedures we were required to follow. His expertise was in an entirely different area and simply wasn't transferable. That didn't seem to have occurred to the executives who appointed him. Nor did it apparently occur to them he might well create a stranglehold on that prized and coveted position for *forty* years. Nor was it realised that his ignorance was not only abysmal but dangerous.

It quickly became apparent that the job was light years beyond his capability. So, as many executive management teams are wont to do, instead of admitting their mistake and putting him on probation, they ordered my two colleagues who'd lost out on the promotion to mentor him.

In their own time.

On their own dime.

In addition to their own intensive and extensive workload.

On the quiet.

Because it wouldn't be a very good look for other departments to realise that ours had an incompetent head. It would bring the entire organisation into disrepute.

My colleagues said no. They stated that, if they weren't good enough to fill the position in the first place, then they certainly weren't good enough to mentor the successful applicant. As for fixing the mess he was making due to his ignorance and inexperience, they told the executive management that was *their* job.

They'd quickly figured out that the new head of department was both entitled and lazy. He had no incentive to learn the routines while he could plead ignorance and farm out tasks to his subordinates. Where once the atmosphere in our department had been collegial and pleasant, now everyone avoided each other and stayed at their workstations during breaks in case they got asked to take on an extra job or even a major additional role.

Very soon the pressure on my colleagues from the top executive to accept all the work the new head attempted to delegate to them was vicious. Management obviously intended to wear them down, hoping they'd crack under the strain and fall into line.

One of them resigned after a few months for a better position in another city. The other kept applying for a transfer to another department and complaining very loudly of discrimination every time he was refused. Finally he got out.

Not only were my two colleagues dispossessed in this process, so was our entire department. In the end, we lost their considerable expertise, experience and that rare, rare ability to work together as a harmonious team.

My social media feed regularly features stories like the one above. Stories where people are deprived of the due reward of their labour; or when people are penalised for doing *exactly* as asked, despite informing their superior of the inevitable disastrous consequences; or where people are told, 'You can't resign. I refuse to accept it. We can't replace you. Where's your loyalty?' when they've found a similar job with half the hours and twice the pay; or when they lost their job for asking for a modest raise and are expected to teach dozens of complex tasks in a few days to their replacement—who, naturally, has been employed at a much higher salary.

It's common for people to be dispossessed in this way. Now you may think *dispossessed* is not the right description. When we talk about dispossession, we often think of loss of inheritance, having a bequest stolen, being ripped off in terms of a legacy, being cheated out of a financial endowment, or being swindled over some property or a sale.

But here in this book, I'm using *dispossessed* in the sense of *being deprived of your rightful calling* or *deprived of a post* for which you are the most qualified, the most experienced, the most proficient and the most dedicated. Sometimes an inheritance, property, legacy or finances may also be involved as part of the background to the theft of your calling. You are manoeuvred into a position as a threshold sacrifice. Your knowledge, hard work, insight and innovative skill are at risk of being used as a sacrificial conduit to 'feed' the company or church or family that is unwilling to raise you up. You're the asset that cannot be unhooked from the feeding tubes, because no one else is willing to put in the over-and-above effort you do.

It's no coincidence that I've just described this kind of situation with words reminiscent of vampirism. Lilith, the spirit of dispossession, is described throughout millennia of history as a vampire.

Now while the dispossessed might feel deep anger at their loss, they are not the only ones carrying hatred. The dispossessor has effectively said: 'I wish you were dead.'

'You are standing in the way of my inheritance.'

'If only you were not here, then this would all be mine.'

Or, if the dispossessor is an authority figure granting a reward to someone who has not worked for it, 'You are opposing my right to bestow this as I see fit. Justice is irrelevant.'

Here we see an alliance with Lilith's alter-ego, Anat, the Canaanite goddess who claimed the right to determine who would rule as king of the gods.

The example I've used above is an inter-generational one. When it's time for one generation to hand over the reins and facilitate a transition of power to the next, then the spirit of dispossession really comes to the fore. It's the natural context for a sudden spike in her activity. Consequently it's not uncommon for an older generation to pass over the next one, and to deny their obvious successors a long-awaited reward for hard work, faithfulness and patient endurance. Instead, influenced by this spirit, the older generation decides to appoint members of a third, much younger, generation as their designated heirs.

Usually, the excuse given for bypassing the middle generation is because they lack creativity. They are therefore said not to be the right fit to take the organisation forward. The older generation conveniently forgets how regularly any suggestions for innovation by the middle generation were stifled and discouraged as too risky or too time-consuming. The middle generation has been waiting for the chance to show how original and inventive they can be, but they've never been offered even the smallest opening.

Not surprisingly, they feel betrayed. They've been deemed unworthy of an inheritance because they haven't demonstrated the very skills that they were actually denied the opportunity to prove. The goal-posts shifted just as they might have expected their turn to lead and they've lost an expected inheritance—sometimes even a birthright—because they've not been seen as forward-thinking.

The younger generation has benefited by the faithful building and quiet obedience of the middle generation—yet perceives them as know-nothings who are blocking the path upward. Ironically, of course, they want their backing and expertise as they step up to take the reins from the older generation. Still, they don't want to give them any more of a voice than the older generation did.

When the middle generation simply pack their bags and leave, both older and younger generations are stunned. They, in turn, feel betrayed. They'd taken the loyalty of the middle generation so much for granted that it didn't dawn on either of them that there'd be a steep price to pay for such gross dishonour and injustice.

The loss of experience and competence—the loss of wisdom, understanding, counsel, knowledge— is precisely what the spirit of dispossession wants. Because then she can step out of the shadows and enter the picture more overtly, offering her own wisdom, understanding, counsel, knowledge and might. She wants us to fear her more than we fear God,[1] and so fall in with her agenda of draining life from others, dispossessing them and depriving them of the fruit and reward of their long labours.

There are, in my view, seven threshold spirits with the ability to block our way into our calling. They mimic the sevenfold Spirit before the throne of God, and they counterfeit a heavenly pattern that they were once very familiar with. At one time they had been throne guardians who held positions where they were in the confidence of God and privileged to be acquainted with His deep counsels.

Because His gifts and offices are irrevocable, they are still able to exercise their privileges when it comes to preventing us from accessing the throne of grace. It's up to us to use our super-admin status as children of God to override these 'denials of service' but we rarely succeed. Instead, we often create such havoc that we're subjected to horrific retaliation when we try to pass over the threshold into our calling.

Now many people don't want to believe threshold spirits exist. The majority of Bible translations quietly encourage us in unbelief: for example, although the name of the spirit of abuse, Belial, occurs 27 times in Hebrew, it's often obscured completely by interpreting it simply as *worthless*.

Yet the consequences of denying the reality of these spirits is that we are nudged, inevitably and inexorably, into dishonour of God. After all, if threshold spirits don't exist, then how do we explain abuse and injustice by the heroes of the faith? Often we decide God approved their violence and cruelty, or we wriggle and squiggle into theological justifications that edge perilously close to blaming God for ruthless brutality. We're like Adam in Eden, when he subtly held God responsible for the first sin on the grounds that, since God created Eve and since Eve fell into temptation first, then it was ultimately God's fault.

As a result of dismissing the existence of threshold spirts, we walk into the battlezones of life, unarmed and unprotected. We assume that God is for us, even while our agreements with these hostile powers limit how much He can stand in harm's way. True, we may not have taken out these agreements ourselves—but covenants, by their very nature, do not disappear when the person who signed off on them dies. They continue until revoked.

Ultimately, if we continue to ignore threshold spirits and their aggressive, antagonistic activities, we implicitly—though usually unconsciously—paint the Father as an abuser. The innocent One has become the perpetrator. What a perfect and triumphal reversal for the spirit of abuse!

Threshold guardians belong, in my view, to the class of fallen angels that Paul called 'exousias' when he described the cosmic opponents ranged against us in spiritual warfare. The Greek word, 'exousias', is variously translated as *authorities, powers* or *rulers*.

> *Our wrestling is not against flesh and blood, but against the principalities, against the powers* ['exousias']*, against the world-rulers of this darkness, against the spiritual hosts of wickedness in the heavenly places.*
>
> Ephesians 6:12 ASV

Paul depicts a hierarchy, with 'exousias' ranking higher than principalities and lower than world-rulers. Where 'archons', *principalities*, rule over cities, regions, territories and nations, the 'exousias' rule over frontiers, borders, fringes, gateways and liminal spaces that define the boundaries between towns or areas, provinces or countries. At least, that's my belief and experience. Moreover, in addition to governing space in the geographical sense, they also have a vested interest in transitions involving time or physical state.[2]

Time, in particular, is a concern of Anat's—especially 'appointed time', that moment decreed by God for us to cast off the old and put on the new. She wants to dispossess us so that the appointed time is completely beyond our reach.

Now sometimes I suspect I'm wrong about the number of threshold guardians. Occasionally I come across evidence of a spirit operating, and I think, 'This is new. I haven't encountered this entity before and it's clearly operating on a threshold.' But further investigation leads me to the conclusion that I've just turned up a new name or an undiscovered face for an old enemy. When I first came across Resheph, I thought I'd have to up my tally of threshold spirits to eight. However, I then realised it was so much like Leviathan it simply had to be one of that dragon's seven heads. Likewise, I concluded that Belial and Kronos were basically the same dark entity.

Such deductions are impossible on the basis of the evidence in Scripture, ancient literature or archaeology. They come out of the practical work of healing and from the realisation that the same 'weapon'—one particular segment from the arsenal of the Fruit of the Spirit—is effective against what seems to be two different foes. It doesn't work, for example, to deploy JOY against Python, the spirit of constriction. LOVE is what overcomes in that situation.

Lilith, too, apparently has a multiplicity of faces—or masks. I will therefore be looking at her under several guises—including the Canaanite war goddess, Anat,[3] and the Greek godling, Kairos. The inclusion of Kairos may come as a considerable surprise if you've been used to regarding that word as simply indicating a divinely appointed moment or a favourable time to take hold of an opportunity.

Lilith wants to spoil the appointed time with untimely destruction. She wants to overturn the moment of achievement and reward through traumatic dispossession.

The language we use to describe our emotional or spiritual pain almost always reveals our attacker. If we mention crushing or squeezing, we're battling Python the constrictor. If we feel we're experiencing backlash or whipping, then our assailant is Leviathan the retaliator. And if we sense we've been staked or speared—as if someone has knifed us in the back, plunged a stake in our heart or skewered a lance into our gut—then it's Lilith opposing us.

Lilith is only mentioned once in Scripture—but then, so is Python. A scarcity of mention in the record doesn't necessarily correlate with a scarcity of presence. Just as it's possible to recognise Python's activity through related words and significant symbols, so too it's possible to detect Lilith as the anonymous spirit at work behind the scenes in particular episodes.

Her sole appearance by name is in Isaiah 34:14. Together with watcher-jackals and goat-demons, she haunts the ruins of the kingdom of Edom.

> *And desert creatures will meet with hyenas, and goat-demons will call out to each other. There also Liliths will settle, and find for themselves a resting place.*
>
> Isaiah 34:14 ISV

Many translations render Lilith as *owl*, since the name derives from night.[4] In keeping with this naturalistic bent, 'sa'iyr' is often presented as *wild goat*, instead of *goat-demon*. This occurs despite its use to denote a *satyr* or *devil* in other contexts.[5] Each of the creatures Isaiah describes has a name with supernatural resonances overlaying natural possibilities. Yes, 'sa'iyr' could indeed be *wild goat*, but it also means *goat-demon*. The word for *hyenas* sounds like the Babylonian for *watcher-angel* used in Daniel's prophecy. It's true that Daniel's watchers are holy ones, however the Israelites tended to associate the term 'watchers' with a group of fallen rebel angels. Furthermore 'lilith' itself evokes—and perhaps was purposefully intended to evoke—the 'lilitu' of Babylonian legend, *disease-bearing wind-spirits*.

Thus, from my vantage point there are far too many overtones of otherworldly, malevolent beings in this verse to consider that Isaiah was merely talking of hyenas, goats and owls. So those translations opting for *night monster, night-hag* or *demon of darkness* as an explanation for 'lilith' seem more accurate to me. This is particularly so when we take the previous verse into consideration.

> *Thorns will grow over its palaces, nettles and brambles its fortresses. It will become a haunt for jackals, a home for ostriches.*
>
> Isaiah 34:13 ISV

Once again, inbuilt double meanings are present in the names of these creatures—and those secondary senses are, again, eerie and unearthly. The word 'tannin' for *jackal* also means *dragon* or *sea-monster*, while 'yaanah', *ostrich*, rhymes with and also encodes 'anah', thought to be the source of Anat, the name of the ferocious Canaanite war goddess—who, in my opinion, is actually Lilith in another guise.

So there's no way in my view that Isaiah meant *owl* when he mentioned Lilith. He was indicating *vampire*.

As if to make up for the scarcity of information in Scripture, tradition and folklore overflow with tales of Lilith's malevolence.

As a vampire spirit, she drains and diminishes our strength by slow stages rather than eliminating us in one swift swipe. Nonetheless she's an opportunist, so if it suits her purposes, she'll single us out for death. However, her preferred option is to feed off our strength. She prefers resurrection life to the ordinary kind. She laps up that life, sapping us dry, depleting us, exhausting us, bleeding us out.

Delilah, the wife of Samson, was probably named after her. Delilah signifies *night*, just as Samson symbolises *day*. Samson comes from 'shemesh', *sun*, and although Delilah is said to derive from 'dalal', *bring low, dry up, be emptied, be impoverished*—reminiscent of all that Lilith does in depleting our strength—her name contains the element 'lel' for *night*.

So on two counts—the association of both Delilah and Lilith with *night*, along with their desire to bring low the strength of others—I believe this is a second, and very extended, reference to Lilith in Scripture. We're shown many of her tactics in the Samson-and-Delilah story.

There are also, in my view, other episodes in Scripture where she is one of the unnamed spiritual powers behind various tragedies. She promotes the outbreak of war, she encourages the escalation of feuds even when various opponents are seeking peace, she's the driving force behind narcissism. She reinforces the blocks making it so difficult for people trapped in narcissism to process shame. As a consequence, they drain others physically, emotionally, mentally and spiritually. She doesn't create the blocks—we do—but she seriously augments them.

Nor does she—at least as far as I can tell—create the 'spear'—the spiritual stake that pins us to a moment of trauma. However once it's been launched at us, she propels it to ensure it's lodged so deep we can't remove it ourselves. Like some other threshold spirits, she is rarely the initiator of trauma—but she is a supremely skilful user of what we put in her hands through our actions and reactions. All too quickly we can become complicit with her agenda—as Samson was with Delilah.

With that figurative spear wedged securely in place—or those knives in the back, skewer in the gut or dagger in the heart—we've got an open wound where Lilith can continually draw life. We may forgive the person who stabbed us, whether physically or metaphorically, and repent of any provocation on our own part—and this removes the spiritual legal right Lilith has to keep a hold on us. However, while the spear is still there, it will draw her back.

Jesus said:

> *'Whenever an unclean spirit goes out of a person, it wanders through waterless places looking for a place to rest, but finds none. Then it says, "I will go back to my home that I left." When it arrives, it finds it empty, swept clean, and put in order. Then it goes and brings with it seven other spirits more evil than itself, and they go in and settle there. And so the final condition of that person becomes worse than the first.'*
>
> Matthew 12:43–45 ISV

Forgiveness and repentance clean up the house of our spirit. However they do not lock the access door against Lilith by removing the spiritual spear that stakes us to the moment of trauma. It's the scent of the still-seeping wound that continually draws Lilith back into our lives, sometimes with other spirits who have accepted her invitation to sip away at the strength God has promised us for each and every day.

Don't you realise that your body is the temple of the Holy Spirit, who lives in you and was given to you by God? You do not belong to yourself, for God bought you with a high price.

1 Corinthians 6:19–20 NLT

The 'house of our spirit' is the temple of the Holy Spirit, our bodies. But we are far more than that temple: we are also the Body of Christ, the Bride of Christ and the New Jerusalem. In the New Jerusalem—the great city, constructed as a cube of jewelled foundations with walls and streets of translucent glass—there is no temple because the Lord and the Lamb are the temple. The glory of the Lord is its light and the Lamb is its lamp. Consider then:

- The Lord God is a place and a person.
- The Lamb is a place and a person.
- We, the people of God and the Bride and the Body, are a place and a person.

This is a difficult concept to grasp within the thought world of the postmodern West, but it's essential to acknowledge it before we go too much further. We don't need to understand it, just recognise that this is the way things work.

Now, besides the Lord and the Lamb and ourselves, there are other entities in Scripture who are also places and persons. In *Dealing with Leviathan*, I pointed out that the multi-headed sea monster God made to frolic in the deep is also a blueprint of the inner court of the Temple in Jerusalem. Actually, Leviathan is more like the furniture in the Holy Place, but the basic principle holds.

Other spiritual beings in Scripture that are, at times, described as places and at other times as persons include Death and Sheol, often partnered together. Sheol is the *grave* or, as often translated, *hell*. That's not a particularly good rendering of its meaning, since *hell* conjures up fire and brimstone when a better description of Sheol is foggy. The passages about the afterlife in Sheol are quite muddled in Scripture but one thing is sure: there's fog of mind and fog of sight, not fire. Now I'm going to suggest, for reasons that will become apparent later, that the primary aspect of the realm of Sheol is blindness. And therefore what Sheol craves, above all else, is sight.

Spiritual sight.

So what does it want to draw into a trap? A seer.

That's where Lilith and Anat—who, by the way, is also a person and a place—come in. Lilith is, after all, the lady of shadows and darkness. Her occult specialty is necromancy—communication with the dead.

Although the traditions about Lilith have changed substantially over the centuries, one aspect has remained constant. She is intensely hostile towards children and babies. She wants to suck adults dry slowly, bringing them down by slow attrition. But with infants it's a different matter. She simply wants them dead.

A lullaby is thought to have originated in a cradle song to ward off her attentions. The word itself allegedly derives from 'lilith-abi', *Lilith begone!*

The earliest evidence for a Lilith-like deity is found in the Mesopotamian legends of Lamashtu, a rogue demon outside the control of the gods, responsible for seducing men, harming pregnant women, killing babies, defoliating plants, drinking blood and bringing disease, sickness, and death.

Lilith is sometimes regarded as the first wife of Adam—however, the first evidence of this legend is in the *Book of Adam and Eve*, an anonymous Christian work based on an Arabic original dating from the sixth century. Also during the sixth century Lilith came to be mentioned several times in the Babylonian Talmud[6] and, from there, she developed into a significant figure in medieval Jewish mysticism. However, her metamorphosis from a baby-slaughtering goddess to the primordial rebel woman took many centuries and only began to happen well over a millennium after Isaiah used the name.

Despite the error in naming Lilith as Adam's first wife, there are nevertheless significant take-aways from this identification. In the legend, Lilith wanted to dominate Adam. And that's a perfect description of this spirit who wants complete and total dominance over the male. She's particularly keen on terrifying male prophets into submission. Sure, she has an agenda towards women too, particularly female prophets. She wants to destroy them or, failing that, terrify them into abandoning their calling so she can feed on them. Men, on the other hand, she wants to dominate. And her track record in this regard, particularly in her guise of Anat, is exceptional.

In addition to this aspect of domination—a dark counterfeit of godly dominion—Lilith leaves other talon-marks in the Adam-and-Eve story. As soon as they'd eaten from the Tree of the Knowledge of Good and Evil, they realised they were naked. In an attempt to process the resulting shame, they hid and covered themselves with fig leaves. But the failure of that approach was evident when they tried to shift the shame away through blame. It was God who eventually gave them a way to process the shame: He 'covered' them.

So too Jesus can 'cover' us. His 'kapporet', *covering*, is the 'kapparah',[7] *atonement*. Our unbelief in the atonement blocks our ability to process shame; and our inability to process shame reinforces our unbelief in the atonement. Lilith empowers this cycle. She doesn't need to get us to deny Jesus to disempower us, she just needs us to believe the lie that the atonement of Jesus is not enough.

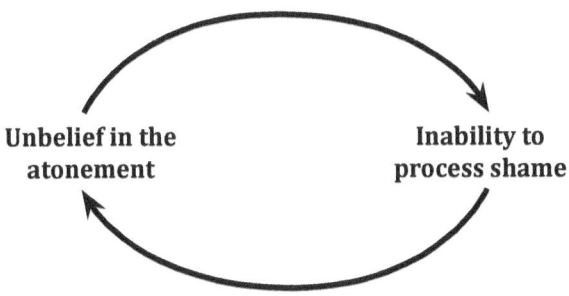

She consequently pushes us *first* into denying the shame, refusing to acknowledge it, so that, *second*, when it is sufficiently repressed that we are no longer aware of it, we can then, *third*—taking a leaf from the classic strategy of the spirit of abuse—attempt to remove the intolerable secret burden by blaming someone else.[8]

Shame attaches to our identity. Guilt attaches to the act of wrong-doing.[9] We feel that guilt can be atoned for, but not shame. Shame-based cultures teach that there is no redemption for it—only exile, hiding or suicide. This is one of Lilith's most profound and successful lies. There has always been covering in Jesus, plus more: there's purification—the removal of the stain of shame.

Jesus gave the woman caught in adultery a way of parsing her shame and moving beyond it. The panic, the dread, the powerlessness and the humiliation she'd have experienced when she was dragged before Him must have been overwhelming. Yet Jesus did not speak words of forgiveness—He did not say, as He had at other times, *'Your sins are forgiven.'*[10] There would have been absolutely no point. Shame is not removed by forgiveness—in fact, forgiveness has no impact whatsoever on it.

Jesus did, however, speak out a curious judgment: *'Neither do I condemn you.'*[11] That wasn't a declaration of innocence for He continued, *'Go and sin no more.'*[12] Yet this wasn't a verdict of guilt either—it's a pardon, a release. There was no condemnation.

This is the secret of removing shame:
> NO CONDEMNATION.

Nonetheless, sometimes we feel self-condemned. But who are we not to accept the pardon of Jesus? Who are we to judge ourselves condemned when the Judge of all the universe has said, *'Go and sin no more'*?

Shame fears to be exposed. It says, 'If you knew who I really am—if you could see the real me—you'd be so utterly disgusted, you'd reject me.'[13] But when the shameful acts are known and not condemned, then true identity can take its first tentative steps out of hiding. Still sometimes people can feel deep conscious shame but, as they search their souls, they can't identify any especially shameful acts. All they really know is that they've *never* not known shame. This, therefore, generally indicates they have taken on the unprocessed shame payload of their ancestors.

There's no doubt in my mind the woman caught in adultery was Mary of Bethany, the sister of Jesus' friend, Lazarus. She was the one who broke open an alabaster jar and anointed Him with nard while wiping His feet with her hair. Given the intensity of cultural shame and the extreme disapproval of the onlookers, I believe there's only one reason she went through with it: she was so far beyond shame she didn't care what anyone thought. As the woman caught in adultery, she'd already been so deeply shamed nothing could touch her again. She wanted to honour the One who'd made her recovery possible. It wasn't that she was shameless, as no doubt most guests thought; she was simply over shame.

And that made her the perfect battle-companion in Jesus' upcoming confrontation with Anat.

Back last century when I was teaching mathematics, a new grading system was implemented across the state education system. It was promoted by university lecturers who knew all the theories but didn't know teenagers. Instead of an ascending 1 to 7 rating scale, with an implied pass at level 4, every student *would* achieve—no matter what. Some would be ascertained as VHA, *very high achievement*, some HA, *high achievement*, some SA, *sound achievement*, some LA, *limited achievement* and some VLA, *very limited achievement*.

Despite the reassurances of all teachers that everyone achieved at some level, no student bought into that thinking. Pass-fail is ingrained in human nature, so why the experts thought this system would work is a mystery. As far as the students were concerned, SA and above was a pass, LA and VLA were, in their opinion, a fail. Nothing would convince them otherwise.

If that had been the extent of the flop in the new system, it might not have mattered. But the worst aspect of the change from number ratings to achievement levels was the automatic and instinctive way that the students adopted a new language about themselves. Whereas in the past they might have remarked, 'I *got* a 2,' now they said, 'I *am* very limited.' No amount of correction or coaxing to say, 'I got a very limited result,' made the slightest difference.

I am is an identity statement, but *I got* is not. One is about *being*, the other is about *doing*. The whole point of the new grading system—to remove the sense of failure from students—backfired in a major way. It reinforced the problem rather than overcame it. It's one thing to fail a subject, it's entirely another to adopt 'very limited' as a defining statement of self.

As the years have passed, university lecturers haven't learned from their mistakes. I'm not even sure they're aware they've made mistakes. Their understanding of teenage thinking or human nature is still superficial and theoretical. Consider one of the latest pushes: the ideology that masculinity is by nature toxic and that boys need to apologise for being male. A momentary spot of reflection might just lead us to the conclusion this is a deliberate attempt to induce shame. But because boys can't effectively stop being who they are, they have no way to process the shame that's manufactured by such teaching.

Lilith can seize this ideal opportunity to drive boys towards narcissism. Then, of course, when full-blown narcissism finally manifests, the teachers will consider themselves vindicated, failing to see that they were actually the driving force propelling the narcissism in the first place. Shame is always traumatic and invariably counter-productive, especially when the threatened person perceives there is no way out of it.

When toxic masculinity is viewed as a set of unacceptable behaviours, then there's a potential pathway for change. But when toxic masculinity is presented as inherent in the male identity, and furthermore men and boys are shamed for it, then more likely than not, it will become a self-fulfilling prophecy.

This is just one example. Skin colour is another. Nationality, ethnicity or ancestry are still others. Whenever we are shamed for something we cannot change, Lilith will snap up the opportunity to tempt us into developing a narcissistic stronghold as our bulwark against life.

Narcissism is shame-based. Addiction is shame-based. Shame is invariably rooted in trauma. Not all trauma, of course, leads to shame—only the kind that seeds and strengthens a core belief that 'I am damaged goods,' 'I'm rotten to the core,' 'I am not only always wrong in what I do, but wrong in my essential being,' 'I'm incurably bad.'

Lilith is willing to use trauma of any kind—whether it's a precursor to shame or not, whether it involves abuse or not, whether it's accidental or not.

The legend of Narcissus is about a handsome young man who fell in love with his own reflection. Completely self-absorbed, he remained in one spot by a pool staring at his image in the water, wasting away until he finally died. Narcissism is named for him. In his tragic story, we can see the symbolic elements that connect up with Lilith: he is stuck in one place, he is slowly drained of life, he is pierced by his own self-image as well as obsessed with it, his world is narrowed into a delusional fixation with a likeness of himself. He's not even truly focussed on himself as himself. Perhaps if he had been, he'd have been able to seek help. His self-centredness is image-focussed. Shame has that effect on us: we want to project the perfect image regardless of our internal destitution.

Shame is, however, the bonus as far as Lilith is concerned when it comes to trauma. She can make use of trauma whether shame is the outcome or not. Trauma is like a spear transfixing us. It pins us, spiritually or psychically, to a moment in time. We tell the same stories over and over—even if it's only in our heads—seeking to process the pain and loss. But, in so many cases, it simply will never make sense. And until we come to acknowledge that it's irrational—and often deliberately so—we will be distracted trying to find reasons for the unreasonable. We'll be mired in the grief of dispossession, unable to move through the stages towards acceptance. We'll focus on the past, bringing it into the present, and seeking by logic to resolve the matter in our hearts rather than turning to Jesus and letting Him work it through. Our very language betrays us—we talk about events that happened decades ago as if they occurred yesterday.

When we do this, we've already fallen for Lilith's most insidious temptations. She says: 'You're resilient, you can work this through yourself, no need to involve Jesus in this one.' Or, alternatively: 'Go right ahead and ask God what the problem is, but then deal with it yourself when it becomes obvious His appointed time is way past the limits of your patience, trust and faith.'

We see this exact scenario happen in the life of King David. It leads him into perpetrating one of the greatest disasters of his life.

Eventually, I want to look at the catastrophe David created. But I want to do so in the context of Anat's influence in Israelite history. Her impact is so devastating, however, it needs to be prefaced with a warning: your faith hero, if you have one, has feet of clay.

> *'Why do you call me good?' Jesus answered. 'No one is good—except God alone.'*
>
> Luke 18:19 NIV

The plain fact is there is only one hero in Scripture. His name is Jesus. *No one is good*, He told us, *except God alone.*

But we don't believe Him. We class our friends and neighbours as 'good people' and speak about them as if they are the norm.

People are complex mixtures of good and evil, light and darkness. However in this world where self-esteem is a societal idol, the words of Jesus that no one is good except God alone are a counter-cultural message. The church isn't bold enough to speak them above a whisper. We instead tend to superglue buffed-up haloes firmly onto various biblical characters, dial up our hero-worship several notches and then promote them as worthy of emulation. We forget that we're supposed to follow Jesus, not Elijah or Joseph, David or Moses. We lower our sights, looking for a human role model because, well, when all's said and done, Jesus is God. So we think He had an advantage that we mere mortals don't. But He was fully human and, not only that, He was tempted as we are.[14] We're not going to face any test He didn't.

I want to stress how important this is before we go on. Otherwise it's going to seem like I'm simply deconstructing all the faith heroes you've been ever taught to revere. Yet Scripture never labels them as heroes; we do. And we do so because of our shame-based fear of being ordinary.[15] That fear is a prime driver of narcissism, and thus compels us to create 'heroes' we can emulate, so we can follow in their footsteps and be heroes too. Scripture, however, is devastatingly honest about the flaws of the patriarchs, prophets and potentates, revealing repeated callous behaviour in all its toxic ugliness. We instinctively sanitise our retelling of biblical stories and our biographical accounts of whatever 'saints' our denomination looks up to. Our blindness to the ruthless, brutal behaviour of so many biblical stars transfers, unfortunately, into everyday life.

Almost every week, throughout the Christian world, there's another high-profile scandal. One recurrent characteristic that crops up time and again in such tragedies is the refusal of a group of loyal supporters to believe the clear-cut evidence of a leader's abuse. One reason I think this happens is because we're taught to see our leaders in the light of these sugar-coated biblical heroes.

The Jewish writer, Bruce Feiler, points out that some detractors of the Bible claim most of it was made up to aggrandise Israelite history and glorify their rulers. Yet, he goes on, such criticism ignores the deep strain of weakness, even criminality, evident in many of the most prominent stories.[16] Christians, far more than Jews, have spin-doctored the abject failures of the patriarchs, prophets and kings to such a degree that some fiascos have become hallmarks of success. We are tolerant of abuse from Christian leaders in part, I believe, because we are so tolerant of abuse in the leaders of Scripture—even though, if we read carefully and in context, God is adamantly opposed to it.

A second reason I think that loyal supporters refuse to believe even the most substantial evidence of a leader's abuse—and tend to treat those who publicly call 'out' the leader's behaviour with verbal or legal violence—is, quite simply, because they are influenced by Anat, the Canaanite face of Lilith. Anat, throughout the epic myth of the Baal cycle, is *insanely* loyal to, and *savagely* protective of, her brother Baal-Hadad. He's the Baal that Elijah confronted at Mount Carmel; and he's one of the faces of the spirit of abuse.

It would be unthinkable for anyone entirely under Anat's sway—or Belial's for that matter—to support the victim. They'll be totally and aggressively behind the perpetrator.[17] This is an extremely sad state of affairs—and doubly so, because we've been brought up to look at biblical figures like Abraham, Joseph and Elijah as little short of idols. Until we realise that the mind control of the spirit of abuse has even influenced the way we read their stories in Scripture, we're not going to be able to deal with the carnage and chaos that Anat and Belial jointly bring into our midst.

Prayer

Heavenly Father, I confess: *no one is good except You alone.*

Lord Jesus Christ, I confess: *no one is good except You alone.*

Holy Spirit, I confess: *no one is good except You alone.*

Blessed Trinity, Father, Son and Holy Spirit, I confess: *no one is good except You alone.*

Father, when I tempted to put anyone on a pedestal, even the men and women of Scripture, remind me: no one is good except You alone.

Remind me constantly, Lord, that people are complex mixtures of good and bad. Remind me, Lord, that faith makes a person righteous in Your sight but it doesn't make them good. Remind me, Lord, that miracles and healings done in Your name are gifts of Your grace but no indicators of the goodness of a person, or even if they know You. As Your Son, Jesus of Nazareth, said: it's by their fruit we will know Your followers.

Lord, grant me the grace to see myself as You see me: not just the righteousness of Jesus but the still, quiet darkness that does not want to be exposed to the light and does not want to bow before You and receive Your blessing for repentance, and Your healing for confession. Grant me also the grace to surrender that darkness within me to You and to come into my calling with Your help. Please rebuke the enemy in all his or her guises on my behalf. I thank You for bringing me this far.

Turn back the enemy at my gates and also on my threshold, and show Yourself strong on behalf of me and my family. Once again, I ask You to sanctify the time as I read on.

I ask all this in the name of Jesus Christ and through the power of His Cross.

Amen

2
Weaving History and Scripture

We need 'Grace' to do the good, and 'grace' to cooperate with 'Grace'.

Austin M. Freeman

ON THE SURFACE, THE SPIRIT of Python seems to be mentioned only once in Scripture—by Luke, when he's describing Paul's run-in with a slave girl in Philippi. Quite possibly you won't even find that. You may search your Bible in vain because Python has been changed from a name identifying a spirit into an occult function: *divination, sooth-saying* or *fortune-telling*. Yet there are eight references to defiled and dangerous thresholds where python is specifically encased in the word for the opening.[18]

Likewise, Belial seems to pop up only once in most English translations. If he's mentioned at all, it's when Paul asked the Corinthians the rhetorical question: *'What harmony is there between Christ and Belial?'*[19]

That's generally the only reference to Belial most of us will be able to find. The twenty-seven instances where Belial is explicitly mentioned in Hebrew are generally obscured by the translation *worthless.*

Apart from Leviathan, threshold guardians are usually hidden—and not by Scripture. The anti-supernatural theological preferences of the majority of translators are the issue. Azazel, the spirit of rejection, might just scrape in, obscured under *scapegoat*, but Lilith is often totally hidden under *screech-owl* or some other creature of the night.[20]

Anat—or Anath—appears several times, but is regarded as so insignificant she can be safely disregarded. I'd never really noticed her before I happened to go through a list of Hebrew words for *time*, looking for the ancient equivalent of the Greek term 'kairos'. Soon it wasn't a can of worms I'd opened, but a can of monsters.

Anat had a profound impact on the history of the chosen people. It's no coincidence that the first miracle of Jesus—the transformation of water into wine at the wedding feast of Cana—is an assault on her. Nor is it a coincidence that the entire interaction between Jesus and Mary Magdalene in the garden outside the tomb is His final and definitive defeat of Anat.

But a defeated spirit is not a dead spirit. Not yet, at any rate.

To understand Anat and thus become aware of our own complicity with her, we've first got to recognise her. Unfortunately, this may involve significant disillusionment regarding biblical figures we've dubbed 'heroes of the faith'. In ignoring their failures and imperfections, we've idolised them. In reality, they were flawed people who are God's instruments for good.

Anat's first major appearance, as far as I can ascertain, occurs in the story of Joseph when Pharaoh has a doublet of nightmares. After his magicians fail to divine their meaning, Pharaoh's cupbearer suddenly recalls a slave he met a few years back when he was in prison—a Hebrew skilled in interpreting dreams. Joseph is quickly made presentable and arrives at the court where, according to all but one of sixty translations, he informs Pharaoh that God will provide an answer. The one exception is the *Names of God* version where it accurately says *elohim* will give Pharaoh the explanation.

Joseph is already politically astute and he uses a highly ambiguous term that could mean *God*, or *gods*, *divine or celestial beings*, *heavenly ones*, *angelic powers*, *goddesses*, *rulers* or *judges*. Whatever Joseph was thinking it wasn't Yahweh—this episode happened centuries before that name was revealed. It follows that, whatever Pharaoh was thinking when Joseph said *elohim*, it wasn't Yahweh either. And as Joseph went on to outline what the dream meant, Pharaoh evidently concluded it was a message from Anat.

This is apparent from his actions on raising up Joseph to be the most powerful man in Egypt after himself. He married Joseph off to Asenath, whose name means *belonging to Neith* or *sacred to Anat*. Neith, *the terrifying one*, is the Egyptian equivalent of Anat.

Pharaoh also called Joseph 'Zaphenath-Paneah'—a difficult name to translate and variously rendered as *saviour of the world, the god speaks and he lives, revealer of secrets*, or *stored beautiful rest*. The first part of the name, in my view, means *Anat of Zaphon*, a recognised title of the Canaanite goddess of carnage and destruction. Anat is often classed as a 'war goddess' but that implies massed armies and orderly strategy far more than it evokes her true nature: a lone warrior in a berserk rage, mowing down even innocent bystanders in a frenzy of insatiable blood-lust.

The last part of Joseph's new name might be a variant on the word for 'face'. This would designate Joseph as Anat's representative. Now through this name-gift, Pharaoh brought a covenant into play. It was one thing to promote Joseph from the prison to the palace, but it was entirely another to do so without any precautions. It would have been recklessly naïve to trust Joseph simply because he was able to interpret the riddling symbolism of a dream.

Name covenants in ancient times had many overtones, but one of their significant aspects was divine insurance against treachery. If Joseph betrayed Pharaoh, then the deities invoked as witnesses would ensure he was executed with extreme prejudice. Importantly, name covenants always involved exchanges. That means Zaphenath-Paneah contains a substantial clue regarding the identity of this seemingly anonymous Pharaoh. Some portion of Zaphenath-Paneah is part of Pharaoh's name.

On that basis, I believe he can be identified as Aperanat, one of the Hyksos rulers—a foreign Canaanite overlord of Egypt in the 15th or 16th dynasty.[21] He too has Anat in his name—thus he would have been brought up to know her saga and liturgy. She was most likely his patron goddess.

Now a seven-year drought occurs in her story. It would therefore have been entirely logical for Pharaoh to conclude that the divinity who was his namesake sent him a warning dream. She'd naturally tell him, as her devotee, of a disaster similar to the one she'd tried to prevent in the Baal Cycle. And what was more reasonable than that her messenger was a slave from Canaan—the land where she was worshipped? In Pharaoh's mind, it probably made sudden sense why the magicians couldn't decode the dream—it needed someone acquainted with the spiritual lore of Canaan to decipher it.

In my view Pharaoh deduced that Joseph was a courier sent to deliver a message from Anat. He therefore honoured Joseph with a wife dedicated to Anat and a new name that reflected one of Anat's titles. But names are not inert labels—they are heralds of destiny. They are portentous and prophetic callings of God. Joseph needed to work through and overcome the claims of the enemy on the identity he was given. In this, Joseph failed. Instead of vanquishing Anat, he fell victim to her.

He became a dispossessor.

I only started to suspect that something was seriously amiss in my understanding of the life of Joseph when I was examining John's gospel. The mother of Jesus, noticing the wine has run out at the wedding in Cana, informs Him of the problem, and then says to the servants: *'Do whatever He tells you.'*

This is a quote. It only ever occurs previously in Genesis 41:55. However, on one level, it's so ordinary it might simply be coincidence that Pharaoh says exactly the same to the starving Egyptians while telling them to go to Joseph for instructions. However John made it clear that he was deliberately evoking the exact moment when Pharaoh put the welfare of the world into Joseph's hands. John did so by a mirror placement of another quote from Joseph's story at the end of his gospel. Jesus, unrecognised by Mary Magdalene, asks her: *'Who are you looking for?'* These same, very ordinary, words occur for the first time in Scripture when a stranger asks Joseph, *'Who are you looking for?'*[22]

Now as soon as I suspected the events at Cana were about Jesus fixing something that involved Joseph, an immediate question arose: *What did Joseph do wrong?* I couldn't think of anything.

Yet Jesus doesn't fix things that aren't broken. The water-wine transformation had to be a reversal of Joseph's wrongdoing. There was a wound that hadn't closed, that was still seeping, that remained infected after nearly two millennia.

I racked my brain but still couldn't think of anything. Sure, there was the obnoxious and entitled arrogance of his teenage years, but that had been beaten out of him in his decade of slavery. I mention this because, in my mind, Joseph was a hero with a halo. And I wasn't even aware I thought of him that way until I had so much trouble trying to understand what Jesus was up to.

Fortunately John had dropped a major clue with those words: *'Do whatever he tells you.'* So, it followed that the problem Jesus was resolving involved whatever Joseph had told the Egyptians to do. The summary in Genesis fortunately couldn't be more succinct. In the first year of the famine, Joseph sold them grain. In the second year, when their money was gone, he took their livestock as payment. In the third year, he took their land and reduced them to bondage.

> *Joseph bought all the land in Egypt for Pharaoh. The Egyptians, one and all, sold their*

fields, because the famine was too severe for them. The land became Pharaoh's, and Joseph reduced the people to servitude, from one end of Egypt to the other. However, he did not buy the land of the priests, because they received a regular allotment from Pharaoh and had food enough from the allotment Pharaoh gave them. That is why they did not sell their land.

Genesis 47:20–22 NIV

Joseph not only reduced the people to slavery, he gave them no way out of it. There was no release after seven years—the land now belonged to Pharaoh in perpetuity—and, in addition, the people had to give one-fifth of their annual produce to Pharaoh. There was no Jubilee year when the land returned to its original owners.

Worse still, according to Jonathan Sacks, Joseph invented the concept of forced resettlement. Sacks translates Genesis 47:21 in line with the Septuagint: Joseph *'removed the population town by town, from one end of Egypt's border to the other.'* [23] In other words, he broke the people's ties to the land that had been handed down, generation after generation, from father to son. The implication is that he provided Goshen—the best of the land, the most fertile allotment in the Nile Delta—for his family by dispossessing the Egyptians. Through this disinheritance he paved the way for the eventual dispossession and enslavement of the Israelites. As

Rabbi Sacks points out, he created the inhumane political mechanism that, in later times, would be used to enslave his own people.

Joseph is not a radiant hero of unalloyed virtue. He was not immune to the song that Anat sang over his life when he was given one of her titles as part of a new name. Did he portray the God of the Hebrews as gracious and compassionate? No, he gave the impression He was a dispossessor, like Anat. And Joseph is by no means unique. So often the dispossessed turn into dispossessors.

Nearly two millennia later, Jesus set about binding up the fracture that still existed as a result of Joseph's actions. We can know that for sure—because, although Jesus created fine, aged wine for the feast, it was also undeniably *new wine*. And *new wine*, as a Hebrew word, is 'tirosh', from 'yaresh', meaning both *dispossession* and *inheritance*.

At Cana, Jesus put Anat on notice He had come to restore all inheritances to their rightful owners. His timing was strategic. The wedding feast was held during the Festival of Tabernacles, the Jewish celebration of Sukkot. It coincided with the last month of the ancient Canaanite calendar, just before their New Year revels—during the same period when Ra'shu Yeni, *first wine*, would have been observed. It was a time when farmers waded knee-deep in grape juice, honouring Anat, who had once waded knee-deep in blood.

Not long ago, I was asked to pray for an indigenous woman who was going to court to try to get back stolen land. She'd been pushed out of her community over a decade previously and, on her return, had discovered various documents covering ownership had been altered. The forces ranged against her were truly formidable: she'd been dispossessed by government agencies, the church, a group within her own family kinship cluster, statutory regulators, lawyers and anthropologists. Privately, I thought her chances of receiving even partial justice were dismal. It would be a miracle to obtain an impartial verdict against even one of those bodies—but *six* miracles!? Nevertheless, I suggested our prayer team treat the issue as one of generational iniquity that could trace its way back to the decision by Joseph to grant his brothers land taken from the Egyptians. I suggested she begin by saying, 'I forgive Joseph for inventing forced resettlement.'

She went on to forgive him for developing the concept of permanent government appropriation of land and for depriving ordinary people of any avenue of appeal. And of course she also forgave, by name where it was possible and appropriate, the government agencies, church, her own family, the statutory regulators, lawyers and anthropologists who had aided the dispossession process. The prayer team asked Jesus to empower her spoken words of forgiveness so they would achieve all He desired of them.

We also acknowledged that, given the cyclical nature of disinheritance and inheritance, although the woman appeared to be the victim, there would be both oppressors and oppressed in her generational stream, both dispossessor and dispossessed, persecutors and persecuted. And that she herself, whether she knew it or not, would carry both. So we asked her to repent of both traits within herself and then we asked Jesus, once again, as our only mediator and advocate to empower the words she had spoken.

It was our hope that, as she went to court a few days later, her submission would be favoured and that, given the complexities of the case and the slow movement of the judiciary, a positive verdict would be made within two years. But just a few weeks later, wonder beyond wonder, God answered our prayers and the land was returned.

The key to this unexpected ruling was treating this situation as if Joseph were part of this woman's personal history, as if he were bloodline kin and forgiving him for a very specific sin. In so much expository preaching today, the designated hero is given a free pass for sin. In fact, over the last few centuries, we've had our consciousness of the sins of the biblical heroes erased.

Now you may think, as you read on and the failures of your favourite heroes are exposed, that it's all too depressing. These dark character flaws are confronting and dismaying. But an important principle to realise is that, because these men and women are part of our family—the family of faith—their actions affect us. Just as Jesus-empowered forgiveness and repentance work to reverse bloodline iniquity, so too they work for faithline iniquity.

An even more important principle to never lose sight of is this: *no one is good, except God alone*. No one. And there is only one unalloyed hero in Scripture. His name is Jesus.

Joseph's awareness of the greatness of God[24] was incredible. He realised God had taken the murderous hatred of his brothers and reforged it to accomplish the salvation of many nations from starvation. Yet in the midst of family reconciliation as well as natural and supernatural blessing, we catch a glimpse of the darkness in Joseph's soul.

In the midst of light, a splinter of night.

And that splinter, unremoved, brought infection to the soul of Egypt. Joseph set up the ideal conditions for a perfect storm of resentment. The indigenous landowners were dispossessed of their inheritance, forcibly resettled so Joseph's brothers and their families could acquire the best grazing country, and suffering under a tax burden that effectively set permanent famine measures in place. They must surely have looked with rage and envy on the wealth, freedom, concessions and land grants given to the foreigners in their midst. Where once Joseph would have been revered for saving the people of Egypt, he would have eventually been loathed for manipulating the circumstances to take their property. Perhaps that festering hatred was the incentive that prompted Ephraim, Joseph's Egyptian younger son, to move to Canaan and establish his family there.

But dispossession was in their blood. Actually, it went back beyond Joseph to his father, Jacob, who dispossessed his twin brother Esau of the birthright of the firstborn. And, it went even further back to Joseph's great-grandparents, who dispossessed Ishmael of the birthright of the firstborn. Six generations down from Abraham, Ephraim's sons didn't buck the trend, they followed it. They decided to rustle some cattle from the inhabitants of Gath and, in the aftermath of the raid, virtually the entire family was wiped out.[25]

Ephraim, however, went on to have more children—a son Beriah and a daughter Sheerah. Now we don't know much about Sheerah. She was born after most of Ephraim's family was massacred, and apart from that, the totality of our direct knowledge about her is summed up in a single verse:

> *His daughter was Sheerah, who built both Lower and Upper Beth-horon, and Uzzen-sheerah.*
>
> 1 Chronicles 7:24 ESV

Sheerah built three cities.[26] In so doing, she challenged the power of Anat, the spirit of dispossession. Sheerah is the first to take up God's promise to Abraham that the land of Canaan is the future homeland of his descendants. She is the first to act on God's word, the first to vest up in the divine inheritance her forefathers had been granted by building a permanent dwelling and moving beyond a nomadic lifestyle.

She built three cities—Upper Beth-Horon, Lower Beth-Horon and Uzzen Sheerah. Beth-Horon means *house of Horon*. He's a Canaanite deity we know virtually nothing about. We do know, however, that he was worshipped in combination with Anat.

Joseph's descendants will always be at the forefront of the struggle against Anat and her allies. Sometimes those descendants will pledge allegiance to her and sometimes they'll raise up a standard against her.[27] It's actually difficult to know what side Sheerah supported in this spiritual battle. Then again, it's often hard to discover what side our own hearts are really on.

Her third town, Uzzen Sheerah, *listen to Sheerah*, is thought to be nuanced *listen to Sheerah's prayer*. She may have been devoted to Anat and Horon or she may have turned to the God of Abraham, Isaac and Jacob.

I believe Isaiah had immense respect for her.[28] He repeatedly alluded to her in his prophecy about renouncing participation in a covenant with Death and with the grave—and how this could change *appointed time*.

Sheerah's achievement is quite stunning when we consider the situation. She believed sufficiently in God's promises to build on difficult terrain in a hostile environment, far away from the support system of relatives living in Goshen. Upper Beth-Horon was built at the summit and Lower Beth-Horon at the foot of a steep incline about 16 km north-west of Jerusalem. It was a long way from help.[29]

Yet her cities remained, century after century—and, while we don't know how successful she was personally in overcoming the spiritual enemy her grandfather had fallen prey to, we do know she laid the groundwork for the success of those who came after her.

Dating the Egyptian Pharaohs and slotting them into a biblical timeline is, at best, contentious. Many historians dispute Rameses II as the traditional culprit during the Exodus. Still, it makes sense.[30] In the following discussion I will be assuming that Rameses the Great is indeed the hard-hearted Pharaoh confronted by Moses and that he died when the waters of the Sea rolled back into place.[31] Most commentators who agree Rameses is the villainous Pharaoh place the Exodus in the middle of his rule, not at the end.

Rameses was in his nineties when he died and he ruled for 67 years. Moses was born eighty years before the Exodus. This places the reign of terror when Hebrew babies were thrown into the Nile during the last years of Rameses I, the grandfather of Rameses II. Horemheb[32] was the childless predecessor of Rameses I. He appointed his elderly vizier[33] as his successor and thus Rameses I was the first ruler of a new dynasty. Consequently, because he was not of Horemheb's bloodline, he was not bound by the covenantal oaths of the past.

> *Now a new king arose over Egypt, who did not know Joseph.*
>
> Exodus 1:8 NASB

The word *know* frequently signifies *covenant* in Scripture. This verse tells us a Pharaoh came to power who was not obligated to keep the covenantal agreement with Joseph. The terms were not simply transferable under a change of dynasty.

It's my belief that Rameses I was the Pharaoh who ordered the slaughter of the Hebrew infants and that it was probably in the last year of his life that Moses was born. Now Rameses' grandson, also named Rameses, would have been in his late teens at this time.

So Pharaoh's daughter—the one who found Moses floating in the basket—could have been the mother, step-mother, aunt, sister, half-sister or even the daughter of Rameses II. Personally I think she was his firstborn daughter, Bint-Anat, a very young girl—not old enough to understand the politics of saving a 'living doll', but still a favoured royal child. Her attendants wouldn't have defied her whims.

Moreover, it would have been much easier for Miriam, tasked with guarding her brother but just a little girl herself, to run up to another child and suggest finding a nurse—rather than approach a powerful adult figure surrounded by a swarm of other adults.

Now my reason for suggesting that 'Pharaoh's daughter' can be identified as the firstborn daughter of Rameses II is because we are told her name in 1 Chronicles 4:17–18. There we learn she was called Bithiah and that she joined herself to the Israelites. She married a man of the tribe of Judah named Mered and bore three sons.

Now, of course, Bithiah and Bint-Anat are hardly the same name. In fact, they couldn't be more different. Bint-Anat means *daughter of Anat*. Rameses regarded Anat as his patron goddess and expressed his devotion by naming his daughter, his dog, his horse and his sword after her.

Bithiah, on the other hand, means *daughter of Yahweh*. And that, frankly, is impossible as her natal-name. No ruler of Egypt worshipped Yahweh. Bithiah therefore changed her name on joining the Hebrew people. What is more probable than that she changed from *daughter of Anat* to *daughter of*

Yahweh? Especially since her firstborn, Miriam, is named after that little girl who was Bithiah's first introduction to the Hebrews.

Bint-Anat was also, by the way, her father's Great Royal Wife—Rameses married several of his daughters, as was a common custom in ancient Egypt. She would have been very old when she left Egypt[34] with her foster-son Moses—ostensibly far beyond child-bearing age. However she would still have been younger than Sarah who birthed Isaac at ninety.

Now the reign of Rameses is too long and complex to examine in detail. Nevertheless I want to point out some relevant aspects when it comes to Anat's legacy in Israel. In the eighth year of his reign, when he was in his mid-thirties and Moses would have been about twenty, Rameses conquered Jerusalem.[35] He also took the city of Jericho before crossing the Jordan and heading north to engage the Hittites. In this campaign he re-asserted control over Canaan. Moses would have been old enough to actually participate in the military operation—and this may explain his puzzling familiarity with the land.

> *When the Lord your God has brought you into the land you are entering to possess, you are to proclaim on Mount Gerizim the blessings, and on Mount Ebal the curses. As you know, these mountains are across the Jordan, westward, toward the setting sun, near the great trees*

> *of Moreh, in the territory of those Canaanites living in the Arabah in the vicinity of Gilgal.*
>
> Deuteronomy 11:29–30 NIV

This comes across as if Moses is speaking from first-hand knowledge.

Now, three years prior to the campaign where Rameses opportunistically conquered Jerusalem on his way to the Hittite Empire, he'd engaged the same enemy at Kadesh in Syria. Once again, Moses could have been involved. Rameses was caught in an ambush at Kadesh but managed to counter-attack and rout the enemy. He was, however, unable to push forward and capitalise on this advance. Although the battle effectively ended in a stalemate, Rameses celebrated it as an unprecedented victory. It was described in hieroglyphics in ten places throughout Egypt. In addition, artistic scenes from the conflict were engraved on monuments at Luxor, Abu Simbel and at the Ramesseum.

One scene portrays the layout of his warcamp. It shows a rectangular tented structure with the same orientation, entrance point, and mathematical ratios in the interior design as the Tabernacle. The instructions God gave to Moses apparently replicate the warcamp of Rameses.[36]

The artwork at Abu Simbel reveals more details: in the exact position paralleling the Holy of Holies is an inner sanctum with kneeling worshippers outside.

Within the inner sanctum is a cartouche with Rameses' name on it, overshadowed by the protective wings of two cherubim-like throne guardians.[37] His cartouche corresponds to the place where the Ark of the Covenant was stationed—he, the god-king, is seated on the equivalent of God's throne.

It gets worse. This is a military camp. And it's at Kadesh—also spelled Qedesh. The word 'kadesh' means *holy*. There are many localities throughout the Middle East with the name. It designates a sacred site where a temple, shrine or cultic object was to be found. However, Kadesh is the name of an obscure Canaanite goddess, often thought to be Anat under a different title: the same Anat who was Rameses' patron goddess of war. His pavilion would have been dedicated to her and it was erected in a location devoted to her.

This raises many troubling questions. Because: when it comes to the Tabernacle and to the Temples that succeeded it, Anat claims to have been there since the beginning. Since *before* the beginning, in fact. As Leviathan is part of the furniture—in the most literal sense—so she is part of the architecture. She asserts all the rights and privileges of millennia of tenancy.

How did this come about? Was Moses so familiar with the Battle of Kadesh and the warcamp of Rameses—either, in reality, because he was there or because the engraved scenes on the stone monuments were so famous—that he naturally thought of the

Hebrew people as the warcamp of God? Did the design elements therefore seep unconsciously into the Tabernacle? Or, alternatively, did Anat aspire to the heavenly Tabernacle and so inspire Rameses to design his warcamp after it? Did she—since she's a threshold spirit and therefore once a divine throne guardian—simply help Rameses duplicate a counterfeit of the royal court of God with himself on the throne?

Either prospect is unspeakably horrifying. I don't really want to face their implications or examine what they mean. Of course, there's always the possibility my timeline wrong and, in fact, somehow Rameses copied the Tabernacle in the wilderness for his warcamp rather than the other way around. But that seems excessively unlikely.

Now, there are two operational factors here: the natural and the supernatural. In the natural, Moses must have recognised the blueprints God gave him. They were too famous in the court where he'd grown up. On the supernatural level, it would not really be a surprise that Anat was copying Yahweh's throneroom. After all, there are little touches in other cultic places that remind us of the Tabernacle—twelve loaves of bread were left on a table dedicated to Ishtar, for example, in temples across Mesopotamia, just as the Bread of the Presence was twelve loaves left on the Table of Showbread.[38]

Now many temples have similar designs, but many more don't. So, it's utterly audacious of Anat to decide to appropriate the architecture of the entire heavenly court. Still, as a long-term war strategy, it's a formidable gameplan. You see, as in the natural, so in the spiritual. By claiming she was first for a design, as opposed to an actual building, she puts a lien on all subsequent constructions. This includes the Tabernacle, the Jerusalem Temple, the land of Israel, the Body of Jesus as the Temple, ourselves as the Body of Christ and the Temple of the Holy Spirit. Legal rights over the first—essentially a copyright or patent—are legal rights over all the rest. God may justly claim a heavenly entitlement, but He didn't enact it on earth before she did.[39]

This is why Jesus never let up on His war against Anat—from the wedding at Cana to the meeting with Mary Magdalene in the garden. Anat had made claims that could not remain unanswered. It's irrelevant that her lien is illegitimate: it needs to be answered. We can't simply ignore the accusations of the enemy, we have to ask Jesus, as our mediator and covenant defender, to answer them on our behalf.

Otherwise, dispossessors gonna dispossess. It doesn't matter that the legal rights of this spirit and her allies are dubious: they're like pushy salespeople to whom *no* means *not now*. If there's any doubt at all that Leviathan or Anat have rights over our bodies as the Temple of the Holy Spirit, they will act as if those rights exist—whether they do or not.

The heart of Moses never entirely left Egypt. To rephrase the old saying, it's much easier to take a man out of Egypt than it is to take Egypt out of the man. Moses not only refused the name covenant God offered to him at the burning bush, some forty years later he was still refusing it when God told him to draw water from the rock by speaking to it. Instead he struck the rock: an action symbolic of refusing covenant. *Drawing water* involves Moses' own name.

Throughout the record, there are constant subtle undertones of Moses holding God at arm's length. God comes to the Tent of Meeting—before the Tabernacle is built—and stands outside, talking to Moses as with a friend.[40] That phrase is one of the most heart-breaking in Scripture: even if we've lost all understanding that this type of covenant is accepted by passing over the threshold, we should still realise that you don't leave your friend standing at the door, you *invite him in*.

At the end of the book of Exodus, there's a remarkable moment when the Tabernacle is finally finished:

> *Then the cloud covered the Tent of Meeting, and the glory of the Lord filled the tabernacle. Moses was unable to enter the Tent of Meeting because the cloud had settled on it, and the glory of the Lord filled the tabernacle.*
>
> Exodus 40:34–35 BSB

Read it again: Moses could *not* enter the Tabernacle. Yet when the cloud of glory had covered Mount Sinai, he was able to enter the cloud—staying there for forty days, neither eating nor drinking. Such an extensive fast isn't necessarily approved by God. God had made it clear, after all, He could provide a banquet—as happened for the seventy elders. By not eating, Moses did not partake in threshold covenant. Nor did he ever offer threshold covenant to God by inviting Him into the tent outside the camp. He'd been totally consistent about refusing threshold covenant for forty years. He wouldn't give up the name 'Moses' with its overtones, *born of the Nile-god*.

His foster-mother Bithiah did what he could not bring himself to do—she gave up her allegiance to the gods of Egypt. Moses repeatedly baulked at accepting a Hebrew name from God, consistently refusing the divine invitation to a whole new identity.

The conflict between Moses and Rameses[41] was also a war between God and the gods of Egypt. In addition, it was a war against Anat—a war for inheritance against the spirit of dispossession.

However, a better role model in regard to Anat is not Moses, but Bithiah. Or Joshua. He, unlike Moses, also accepted a change of name. Originally he was Hosea, *salvation*, but Moses dubbed him Joshua, *Yahweh is salvation*. Yes, irony of ironies, it was Moses' choice.

For over a century the city-states of Canaan had been under the control of the Pharaohs. Despite conquering Jerusalem and Jericho, Rameses basically *re*-established Egyptian rule over Canaan—he didn't establish it in the first place. This was probably why Moses fled to Midian after killing the Egyptian overseer, rather than Canaan where all the local kings were vassals of the Pharaoh.

Now Joshua led the people across the Jordan to take up their promised inheritance almost exactly forty years after they'd left Egypt. So it was nearly forty years since the death of Rameses II. Pharaohs had come and gone—a half dozen as a matter of fact. The seventh of them had come to power. His name was, not surprisingly, Rameses III.

At this point the ruler of Jerusalem was sending frantic messages to Egypt about the incoming Hebrews. Scripture calls him Adoni-Zedek, *lord of righteousness*. That's usually considered a title, rather than a name. His name was almost certainly Abdi-Heba—attested in correspondence with Egypt where he was pleading desperately for help against the invaders. Abdi-Heba means *servant of Hebat*, a little-known Hurrian goddess regarded as the equivalent of the even lesser-known Hittite goddess Hannahannah but who, in turn, has many characteristics in common with Anat.

What else were we expecting? Of course, the fight was against Anat. The dispossessor doesn't want anyone to take up their designated inheritance. Now, of course, it wasn't *just* against Anat. Other threshold guardians had regrouped since their defeat at the parting of the Red Sea.

Joshua was a descendant of Joseph. He hailed from the tribe of Ephraim and was a distant relative of Sheerah. So, if anyone was tasked with taking up the war mantle and opposing Joseph's namesake, Anat of Zaphon, Joshua was certainly in line. He met her claims—not just that she is the ultimate combat champion but that she rules appointed time—and he dismissed them in an utterly superlative victory. And he did so not long after a disastrous mistake.

Moses had repeatedly urged the people to go to Shechem and reaffirm their covenant with God near the great trees of Moreh where Abraham built his first altar in the Promised Land. It's then and there that Joshua's mistake occurred. Not many days after the recitation of the covenantal blessings and curses some envoys from Gibeon turned up, asking for a treaty. Now the Israelites had been told by God not to make a covenant with the locals, but the Gibeonites pretended they'd come from a far country. Too late the Israelites discovered the deception. By the time they did, they were obligated to defend the Gibeonites for all generations, come what may.

The covenant was soon tested. The ruler of Jerusalem, no doubt the one who repeatedly asked Pharaoh to send troops to repel the Hebrews, sent messages to four other local rulers. The plan was to come down hard on the alliance between the Gibeonites and the Hebrews. Abdi-Heba—or, as Scripture titles him, Adoni-Zedek— appealed to the kings of Hebron, Jarmuth, Lachish and Eglon to join him in attacking Gibeon.

The Gibeonites promptly sent for help from their new allies. Theirs was an interesting dynamic, often utilised by the spirit of abuse: we lied to you, we deceived you, we manipulated you, but come and rescue us. After all, we expect you to keep your promise.

The Israelites responded to the call, marching all night to surprise the five armies besieging Gibeon. A rout followed. The five armies scattered, fleeing along the route to the coast. As they did, Joshua realised the need for a comprehensive defeat. If he allowed a sizable portion of the opposition to escape, he'd be asking for trouble. They would be able to regroup, bring in reinforcements, and attack the Israelite camp where the women, children and elderly would be vulnerable.

So, in an outstanding display of faith, he prayed for the sun and the moon to stand still—and thereby give his troops time to finish the battle. In other words, he asked God for the appointed number of hours in a day to be changed. The substance of his declaration was for God to show Himself more powerful than those of His spiritual enemies who claimed to govern time.

Now the place where Joshua asked for this time-bending miracle was the path up the slope between

Lower Beth-Horon and Upper Beth-Horon. If you recall, they were the first cities built by a Hebrew in the land promised to Abraham. Ephraim's daughter Sheerah had placed her faith in God's oath and erected twin cities in this location. She gave them the same names: thus she constructed a city cut into two parts. She modelled a covenant in her townplan and then raised it in the landscape. And in that sacred space, Joshua called on God for an unprecedented miracle.

Now this presents us with an intriguing possibility: Sheerah's architectural design is for a sacred space where Anat not only has no claim, but where she was defeated. Isaiah recognised this, and called it into being. It's far too easy to become so temple-focussed that any other blueprint is unthinkable. Yet that time-bending miracle in the days of Joshua was just the first of its kind—it happened again in the time of Isaiah. In fact, Isaiah prophesied it *would* happen—a stunningly brave prophecy when we consider the likelihood of time stopping or reversing—so long as the people renounced their ungodly covenants and followed Sheerah's design principles. If they did, then God's new cornerstone in Zion would result in the same victory over besieging armies, the same influx of stones from heaven, the same alteration in the flow of appointed time.

These are speechlessly amazing victories—but in both instances, follow-up was lacking. That was the critical error.

Abdi-Heba had written several plaintive pleas to Egypt. One missive said: 'As the king has placed his name in Jerusalem forever, he cannot abandon it—the land of Jerusalem.'[42] This is an enormously significant statement. Which king did this? It's unlikely to be Rameses III. But perhaps Rameses II placed 'his name forever' in Jerusalem when he conquered it a century earlier. Was this why Abdi-Heba worded his appeal this way—fundamentally saying it wouldn't be a good look for Rameses III to lose what Rameses II had won? And if this is the case, what witnessing deities would Rameses II have called on when he made such a pact? He wasn't just devoted to Anat—he also claimed Horon as a protector.

Ironic, then, that the ruler of Jerusalem was one of the five kings who escaped Beth-Horon and hid in a cave, only to be taken out and executed. Despite disposing of the rulers, Joshua did not follow up by taking the city of Jerusalem. He focussed on taking the fertile areas, leaving pockets of Canaanites—now free of Egypt, by the way—throughout the land. Jerusalem, at least in Joshua's time, wasn't considered a prize worth having: it was on the edge of the desert and its water supply was meagre. It wasn't until David saw its potential centuries later that the Jebusite fortress fell into the hands of the Hebrews—and, even then, it was partial possession. David, after all, bought the threshing floor of the Jebusite king, Araunah—a sacred place where worship was offered, divination was practiced, judgments were made and treaties were signed—all with various pagan deities involved. David saw the power—not the problems—of the site.

Isaiah, on the other hand, was far more clear-headed about the spiritual payload involved. He considered the mess so unfixable that nothing less than a new cornerstone—a completely new beginning—was needed. God had proclaimed Jerusalem to be *'the city where I chose to put My Name,'*[43] and who consecrated the Temple *'by putting My Name there forever'*[44] but the people of Israel were still acting as if Anat had the superior claim.

It was unfortunate that Joshua wasn't aware of Jerusalem's pre-eminent status in this regard. He apparently thought the place where God had chosen to put His name was Shechem. That was, after all, where Moses had directed covenant blessings and curses be pronounced from the mountains of Ebal and Gerizim. Considerably over a millennium later, the woman Jesus met at the well in Samaria was still of that particular view.

Joshua built an altar on Mount Ebal according to the instructions in the Book of the Law. Moses had repeatedly directed the people to go to the place where God had put His name—but he did not specify its location. He did not mention Jerusalem at all. He is vague:

> *Instead, you must seek to enter only the place that the Lord your God will choose among your tribes. There He will establish His name and live.*
>
> Deuteronomy 12:5 ISV

Just a half dozen verses later, he reiterates

> *Then to the place the Lord your God will choose as a dwelling for His Name—there you are to bring everything I command you: your burnt offerings and sacrifices, your tithes and special gifts, and all the choice possessions you have vowed to the Lord.*
>
> Deuteronomy 12:11 ISV

Again, he doesn't specify where this place is. In fact, despite repeated instructions of this kind, he never pins the location down. And, although in hindsight we naturally gravitate towards Jerusalem as the answer, I simply cannot imagine that, if Joshua had had even the slightest inkling of this, he would not have moved the stars as well as the sun and moon to take and occupy it as a priority.

Instead he set it up on Mount Ebal at Shechem. And over the following centuries the Tabernacle moved from Shechem to Mizpah to Shiloh to Nob to Gibeon to Jerusalem and, until it became a static fixture in the Temple, no one apparently thought twice about its ability to pick up its tent pegs and move. It's quite easy to forget in all the songs of praise and dances of joy celebrating Jerusalem that it has a depraved side too. In his vision of things-to-come, John the elder describes the martyrdom of the two end-time witnesses:

> *Their bodies will lie in the public square of the great city—which is figuratively called Sodom and Egypt—where also their Lord was crucified.*
>
> Revelation 11:8 NIV

Sodom and Egypt. They are not sudden new infiltrations as the return of Jesus approaches, they have been there since the beginning.

Joshua made extraordinary strides against Anat but, in the end, he did not clear her influence totally out of the land. Jerusalem reverted to a Canaanite enclave, Jebus. The Egyptian outpost of Beit She'an remained. Anat was worshipped there as the Queen of Heaven—in fact, the precinct of the Ashtoreths where, a few centuries later, Saul's armour was displayed after his death may be her temple.

The land of Israel—the great inheritance God had promised to His people—was like a body riddled with pockets of disease.[45] Healing was only possible through undivided loyalty to Yahweh. But that wasn't happening any time soon—in fact, it still hasn't happened.

After the death of Joshua came the era of the Judges when *'everyone did what was right in his own eyes.'*[46] The third judge was Shamgar ben Anath—Shamgar, *son of Anat*. We know so little about him it's difficult to discern whether this Anat is a person, a place, the goddess or a brotherhood of warriors. Such idiomatic uses of 'ben' to mean a guild[47] or band rather than a biological child include 'bene hannebim', *the sons of the prophets*, meaning a company of prophets, and 'bene ha'elohim', *company of angels*.

Shamgar killed 600 Philistines with an ox-goad, a feat that indicates he was highly trained in combat skills and could adapt farm implements into weapons. It also suggests he may have been able to pump up his adrenaline to an unstoppable berserker-like rage. He was a contemporary of Deborah.

She lived in the hill country of Ephraim—indicating she was probably another of Joseph's descendants. The Canaanites had once again become a formidable force, particularly those from Hazor in Upper Galilee. Their cavalry boasted nine hundred iron chariots— the type that had three riders each—and their army would have numbered thousands more.

Now Deborah held court under a palm tree. People came from all over Israel to receive her judgments. It's unclear whether she was the wife of Lappidoth, *torch*, or whether she simply had the title 'torch-bride'.

Even before she got to battle, the *torch* and her office as a *judge* mark her out as Anat's arch-opponent. The story of Deborah and Barak isn't so much a war against Canaanite oppression as a war against their gods. Anat was deemed a torch of the gods as well as a judge of both gods and mankind by the sun-goddess

Shapash.[48] Anat was helped by Shapash to rescue Baal-Hadad from the underworld.[49] Baal-Hadad was the storm-god, cloud-rider and lightning-wielder.

Not coincidentally, Barak's name means *lightning*. This reinforces the picture of spiritual warfare against the Canaanite pantheon. Barak counterpoints Baal-Hadad, the brandisher of lightning, while Deborah counterpoints Baal's warrior-sister, Anat. Perhaps Barak's reluctance to go to war without Deborah at his side indicates his fear of the war goddesses[50] worshipped by the Canaanite commander, Sisera. Perhaps it also testifies to a heart-belief that, because of the involvement of those goddesses, he needed a woman to make victory possible.

When—against impossible odds—that victory came to pass, Deborah sang:

> *In the days of Shamgar son of Anath...*
> *travellers took to winding paths.*
> *Villagers in Israel would not fight;*
> *they held back until I, Deborah, arose,*
> *until I arose, a mother in Israel.*

Judges 5:6–7 NIV

That last phrase 'a mother in Israel' is another parallel with Anat, the 'mother of gods'. A further correspondence involves Anat's Egyptian counterpart, the goddess Neith,[51] who was often depicted wearing the crown of Lower Egypt. This woven crown was adorned with a stylised probiscis to symbolise a *bee*—one of the meanings of Deborah.

In her victory song, Deborah mentions the stars fighting against Sisera.[52] It may be a literal reference or possibly metaphorical.

> *From the heavens the stars fought, from their courses they fought against Sisera.*
>
> Judges 5:6-7 NIV

This could indicate a hailstone or meteorite strike, similar to the shower that aided Joshua in his battle with the five kings. Or, alternatively, it could be an astrological reference. The Canaanites believed in following signs from the heavens. Thus, there would have been an 'appointed time' for victory.

Deborah makes it clear in her song that God rules the stars and makes the decrees for the appointed times. Her clansman Joshua summoned time to do God's bidding; she followed his footsteps. She is the first figure classed as a prophet who shapes history through the delivery of a word from God. Appropriately another meaning of her name, besides *bee*, is *word*.

Apart from Isaiah, Deborah is the only prophet to declare that the appointed time is God's to determine and that a petition to Him can alter the hour of its arrival. She would have been there, egging Mary on, at the wedding feast of Cana. She was definitely not of the view of so many later prophets that Anat was far too frightening and powerful to oppose.

She reveals God's strategic plan for us with regard to Anat. Barak gathered ten thousand men at Mount Tabor. Yet they didn't have to fight—they just had to mop up after God sent a flood against the enemy. So it is that we are not called to engage with Anat and her allies—it's our role to draw the enemy out, so God can fight on our behalf.

Deborah's story is *almost* the last time—until Jesus arrived on the scene—that Anat suffered a major defeat. In the next millennium, there'd be just one more time. It's rather a depressing picture. Not because Anat can't be defeated— obviously she can— but because so many people of God fell by the wayside.

Samson was a champion of Israel during the time of the Judges. For forty years, the Hebrew people had been oppressed by the Philistines—seafarers from the Aegean who had occupied the southern coastal strip and formed a confederacy of five cities. This powerful and hostile alliance was Samson's foe throughout his lifetime.

Samson's name means *man of the sun*. Delilah means *daughter of the night*. Her name is related to Lilith. By the time he met her, he'd been married to a Philistine woman who'd been killed in retaliation for one of his raids. But that hadn't stopped him baiting the Philistines. He'd become exceptionally cunning at both annoying and out-manoeuvring them. He'd visited a prostitute in Gaza and then managed to save himself by manipulating threshold covenant to his own advantage. When the citizens of Gaza realised their enemy was in town, they decided to wait outside the city gate to kill him. Seeing them there, he'd ripped the gates from their posts and carried them off, all the way to Hebron. There's no doubt the men of Gaza *could* have killed him, but they had too much integrity to do so while Samson was 'inside the gate', extending the covenantal protection of the city as he walked along. He taunted them with his strength and his trickery. The shame he inflicted on the citizens of Gaza was intolerable. Both their friends and enemies would have dissolved into mocking laughter at this tale of Samson's ingenuity.

Samson was resourceful, intelligent and hyper-strong. Often he's presented as somewhat dim-witted—completely unable to see through Delilah's blandishments. She's almost always seen as another Philistine bride—yet the text doesn't say that. She lived very close to Jerusalem. The Philistines went to her and offered her, in today's money, $54 million to find out the secret of Samson's strength. And because she eventually winkles it out of him, she is seen as the seductress who betrayed him into the hands of those citizens of Gaza who'd been aching for revenge ever since that excruciating embarrassment over the gates.

Yet is Delilah simply a tool of the Philistine rulers? Why did they offer so much money, if she's one of their people?

Now you can't tell me that, after the second time Delilah has tied him up while he's asleep and then has cried out in warning, *'Samson, the Philistines are upon you!'* that he doesn't know the score. He's not that stupid. Nor is he that naïve. The entire history of his interactions with the Philistines testifies to that. He might have been gullible and credulous in the days of his first marriage, but that time is long gone.

I think there's a strong possibility that, once again, Samson had set up the Philistines. He and Delilah may well have colluded in a scam together. $54,000,000 is, after all, a serious temptation. She could pretend to sell him out and he could pretend he knew nothing of the scheme. They'd make an absolute fortune together. And Samson, unfortunately, was that shameless—remember the prostitute. If he could get away with it, his humiliation of the Philistines would be complete. There'd be no reason for him to think that revealing the secret of his power, and risking the cutting of his hair, would make any real difference. He'd broken his Nazarite vow several times and none of those breaches[53] had any apparent effect on him. The revelation of his secret is therefore not careless, but arrogant.

The Hebrew wording makes it clear that the two incidents—the loss of the gates and the loss of his hair—are linked. Samson took their *gates* (sha'ar), and the Philistines took his *hair* (sha'ar). Samson therefore reaped what he'd sowed: he'd humiliated the people of Gaza; they humiliated him. He made them a mockery, they made him a mockery. And he died pushing down two pillars in a temple, just as he had once ripped up the pillars of the city's gates.

In my view—whether Delilah betrayed Samson without his knowledge or whether they connived together to cheat the Philistines—there's no escaping his complicity with her. The only question is: was it conscious or unconscious? Deliberate or unintentional?

Samson's loyalty to Yahweh was seriously defective. His collaboration with Lilith, the spirit behind Delilah, is plain.

All too often, Christian leaders are like Samson. They despise the grace of God, relying on His power despite their involvement with prostitutes or sexual immorality, despite breaking vows and commitments to Him and to others, despite their manipulation of the integrity of both believers and non-believers, despite their scheming partnerships to swindle those who trust them. When leaders see that the gifts of God are irrevocable, and are unaffected by their hypocrisy and secret sin, they ignore His tender appeals, His kind rebukes, His harsh reprimands and finally His removal of protection. They continually intensify their wrong-doing.

Lilith empowers the cycle with shame. She'll even use God's word—meant to convict us and draw us back to Him—as a weapon to shame us. At some point, the prospect of exposure is too much to contemplate. And that's when Lilith is there with a deal, offering safety. We get to hide the shame with self-righteousness[54] and narcissism, to medicate it with the forgetfulness of addiction.

All Lilith wants in return for this kind of deal, this truce, this agreement, is our inheritance. She wants to drain us of resurrection life so we cannot enter our calling. She wants to push out the appointed time for us to attain our destiny so far it is beyond our lifetime. She doesn't just want to suck us dry, but all the generations that come after us.

Samson is not the only champion of Israel who had a desire to outwit the Philistines, play them for dupes and take advantage of a threshold covenant with them. David does the same, and with less justification. David was on the run from Saul and made up his mind to seek shelter with the Philistines. He took his wives and family, and pledged allegiance to the king of Gath.[55] That's the city that Goliath came from. There are subtle reminders of Samson's visit to Gaza in David's interactions with the Philistines of Gath.

David had already fled there once previously—and had to pretend he was insane in order not to be seen as a threat. He drooled and clawed the doors, and was eventually thrown out of the palace. But not killed. The Philistines knew who he was and yet didn't seek reprisal for the death of Goliath. Within their city, he was protected by threshold covenant—and, like the men of Gaza frustrated by Samson's action in extending the covenantal protection of the city by moving the gates, they kept their pledge of peace within the town boundary. The Philistines exhibited an honour and integrity that neither David nor Samson did.

On his visit to Gath a second time, David had the effrontery to tell the king he would take up arms against his own people.[56] His intention was deceptive from the get-go. Pleased with such a formidable ally, the king gave him the fortress of Ziklag as a base. From there, David and his band of mighty men raided the allies of the Philistines, making sure he never left any survivors. He didn't want to take the chance his deception would be revealed.

Eventually, he became the armour-bearer of the king—meaning that, whatever covenants may or may not have been sworn beforehand, there was certainly one in place when he took up that role. He was now in an invidious position: he had a covenant with Achish, king of Gath, as his armour-bearer; he had a covenant with Saul, king of Israel, as his armour-bearer; he had a covenant with Jonathan, crown prince of Israel, as a blood-brother and covenant defender; and he had a covenant with Michal, Saul's daughter, as his wife.

These covenants don't come into conflict unless there's a war between the Israelites and the Philistines. And of course there was.

Fortunately, on the way to the battle, the other Philistine rulers objected to David's presence. They suspected he might turn on them in the midst of the fray and so wanted him and his band gone. Reluctantly and courteously Achish sent them off, releasing David from his covenantal obligations.

David went back to Ziklag and discovered that his base had been raided—all the women and children have been abducted by the Amalekites. He then does a curious thing: he asks the priest, Abiathar, to use the ephod to inquire of the Lord whether to pursue the raiders or not. On the face of it, a decision to go rescue all the wives and children is a no-brainer. What was so difficult about that choice that it required an answer from God?

The fact is, David did *not* want to take responsibility for this decision. *Whatever* he chose, it was going to be *wrong*. He should not have been at Ziklag to even know there was trouble there. He should have been at Mount Gilboa, keeping covenant with Saul and Jonathan. He should have prevented Saul from his desperate and disastrous consultation with the ghost of the prophet Samuel. Had he been there, Saul would probably not have sought the aid of the bottle-mistress, the witch from Endor. A covenant with Death and with Sheol, *grave*, was emplaced over the nation through necromancy—divination through consultation with the spirits of the dead, an occult speciality of Lilith.

Just as the Philistines praised their high-god Dagon for delivering Samson into their hands, so they praised him for the death of Saul—hanging Saul's head in Dagon's temple. His armour went to the temple of the Ashtoreths in the city of Beit She'an and his body was affixed to its walls. The Ashtoreths are thought to be the sisters, Astarte and Anat. Having made an agreement with Sheol and with Lilith the night before the final battle, it should not be unexpected to find his armour becomes a trophy of Anat.

Saul is completely responsible for his actions and choices in seeking the help of a medium and occult forces. It's irrelevant that David wasn't there to stop him. However David's obligations to Saul and Jonathan were not thereby nullified.

In avoiding responsibility, there's an element in David's use of the ephod to blame-shift onto God. Back in Eden Adam had tried to side-step accountability: *'the woman that You gave me'* is a subtle accusation directed at God. Here we see David following the same path. He got himself into a double-bind because he'd made the unwise decision to seek refuge in Gath.

Saul's participation in necromancy at Endor shows that his loyalty to Yahweh continually wavered. And despite those beautiful psalms, David's loyalty wavered too. Not so much perhaps, but it certainly wasn't unadulterated. He could have rescinded the agreement with Sheol and the grave that Saul made on the night before he died but, instead, he reinforced it.

And it was not removed until Jesus brought Lazarus back from the dead.[57]

It's always Jesus. Always Jesus.

It doesn't matter if it's Adam's sin in Eden, Noah's curse on Canaan, Abraham's inaction when it came to abuse, Rachel's theft of her father's idols, Joseph's dispossession of the Egyptians, Saul's covenant with the grave, David's failure to keep his oaths, Rehoboam's loss of an undivided kingdom, Elijah's neglect of God's instructions, Nehemiah's expulsion of foreign women—Jesus is onto it. But do we notice Him mending anything apart from Adam's sin? Because all too often we've rationalised iniquity committed by our designated heroes, justifying it because the villains need to be opposed, we don't realise there's anything to be fixed. We therefore don't notice when Jesus sutures the wounds of history. As a consequence, we not only underrate His life's work, we miss the moment when God's judgment becomes apparent. We think God approves because Scripture appears to be silent, and lacking in condemnation. The verdicts of the Father are, however, written in the life of Jesus.

He remastered the old stories, changing darkness and depravity into light and hope. He continually worked and prayed to give us back the inheritance we had lost. He was in constant conflict with Anat. As we look back through the pages of Scripture, it becomes clear this is a war for the soul of civilisation. It's not simply for our own individual souls, or for our family's generational inheritance, or for our community or nation. Ultimately it's for what it means to be civilised—to treat each other with honour and respect, to do unto others as we'd have them do unto us, to love our enemies and do good to those who hate us.

Anat is not simply a thief of inheritance, she's a wrecker of civilisation. She wants a return to chaos, through anarchy and war.

A society becomes a civilisation when it moves towards protecting its weaker and more vulnerable members; providing specific areas of safety for them; respecting and honouring differences rather than viewing them as a threat—when it does not take benefits from one member at the expense of another, or perpetrate injustice to redress an inequality or imbalance. Instead it lifts everyone up together. In the early twenty-first century we are seeing more than culture wars and more than the breakdown of society, we are witnessing attempts to destroy more than three thousand years of civilisation.

The war between chaos and order is one we face in opposing Leviathan, but the war between anarchy and civilisation is much more complex. That's the battle we enter when we start to oppose Lilith and her counterparts: Anat, Athena, Neith, Hannahannah, Hebat, Inanna, Ishtar, Minerva.

David's reign opens with a violent rip in the fabric of civilised behaviour. It starts with human sacrifice. David isn't responsible for this event, but it casts a long shadow over his kingship. He duplicates a similar sacrifice towards the end of his reign in the same location—and he never forgives his nephew Joab for what happened in the aftermath of the initial momentous day.

David left Ziklag and settled in Hebron. There he was anointed king over Judah. Meanwhile Ish-bosheth,[58] the son of Saul, was anointed king over Israel and was residing east of the Jordan. Ish-bosheth's armies were scouting around Saul's former capital[59] Gibeon at one point and happened to arrive just as David's armies under the command of Joab marched up.

It's important to reconstruct the backstory since it's so central to ongoing events. Saul's original base was his hometown Gibeah, but he apparently moved to Gibeon—a distance of seven kilometres.[60]

Now Gibeon in the early days of Saul's kingship was a strange mix. These days we'd class it as cosmopolitan: Canaanites, Philistines and Israelites all resided there. It was actually a Canaanite enclave within the territory of Benjamin; its inhabitants were descended from those Hivites who'd deceived the Israelites during the days of Joshua and wangled themselves a covenant.

Curiously a Philistine garrison had also been established there. More curiously still, it was a Levitical city—one of the scattered communities of priests who had not received any specific territorial allotment in the distribution of land during Joshua's time. When we consider this apparently peaceful mix of Levites, Philistines and Canaanites, and also take into account David's relationship with Achish, the king of Gath, we can see that the Israelites and Philistines weren't always at each other's throats.

Now there was a high place at Gibeon. Until the Temple was built at Jerusalem, this was where the kings worshipped at the Tabernacle. Saul, David and Solomon all went there. The Tabernacle was apparently located at Gibeath ha'Elohim, often translated *hill of God*, but in my view probably meaning *hill of the angels*.[61]

Now this set-up makes practical sense. The Gibeonites, under the terms of the ancient covenant with Joshua, were required to be hewers of wood and drawers of water for the sacrifices of the priests serving at the Tabernacle.

At some point Saul had massacred the Gibeonites. While it's not recorded in the events of his reign, it was revealed to David, when he sought the Lord many years later, that the reason for a prolonged drought and accompanying famine was Saul's breach of covenant. Under the terms of the old treaty, the Israelites were required to protect the Gibeonites. Instead, Saul had slaughtered them.

Now while Scripture doesn't mention the exact circumstances of this massacre, I think it's possible to reconstruct the situation. The most likely scenario, given there's no reference to this genocide prior to David's message from God, is that it happened during a wide-ranging battle involving so much killing that the significance of the Gibeonite massacre was completely overshadowed. Such a conflict is indeed recorded: it's the famous battle initiated by Jonathan and his armour-bearer in scaling a cliff near Michmash and attacking a Philistine outpost. By the time Saul and his army joined in the fracas, the Philistines were in full flight back along the road towards the coast. The Israelites pursued their retreating enemies as far as Aijalon. And to reach Aijalon, they had to pass Gibeon where that Philistine garrison was stationed.

Now no one with any sense of military strategy would have failed to seize that stronghold. Otherwise they risked being attacked from the rear as they moved on. In taking this garrison during a battle that swept across almost half the width of present-day Israel, it's apparent Saul's army didn't discriminate between Philistine and Canaanite. They simply didn't stop to ask questions—they eliminated anyone who was not clearly a Levite.

Gibeon was a prime piece of real estate. Well-fortified, with the Tabernacle in its environs, it makes perfect sense for Saul to have moved his capital there. It was within the territorial allotment of his own tribe, after all.[62]

So, there those armies of David and Ish-bosheth were, in sight of the Tabernacle with possibly a Levite or a water-carrying Canaanite wandering around. Rather than attack each other, the armies sat down around the Pool of Gibeon and eyed each other off. Then Abner suggested a game. 'Let's have a laugh': that's what the Hebrew says.[63]

Abner's bizarre idea of a bit of fun was to appoint twelve representatives from each side, have them line up and face each other, then grab their opponent's hair and stab them in the side. Inexplicably, Joab agrees to this unusual sporting competition. Once the game is over and twenty-four young men are dead, it's as if the armies wake from a collective trance. A battle begins.

Abner makes a run for it. However, he's followed by Asahel, Joab's younger brother. Abner pleads with Asahel to stop the pursuit and, when he won't, Abner puts a spear through him and he too dies. This is the beginning of a blood-feud between Joab and Abner.

Lilith is not the only spirit involved in this story, but she's the one we'll focus on. She's the one who spears, stabs, stakes, pins, injects, spikes, knifes, impales, needles, pierces. Abner's 'game' has all the overtones of ritual sacrifice associated with the Greek godling of opportunity and appointed time, Kairos. In Christian circles today, 'kairos' tends to be deep-clean sanitised so the word no longer carries its ancient overtones of offering up a young and unspoiled victim to win favour with the deities of Time. Its roots, nonetheless, are in 'seizing Time by the forelock' and striking a killing blow at a vulnerable part of the body.

What fun, eh?

Were Abner and Joab each sacrificing a band of twelve young men to try to appease the spiritual powers of Gibeath ha'Elohim? Did they think of this site where the Tabernacle was situated as the *hill of God* or the *hill of the angels*? Were they trying to win the kingship for their own candidate by this means? Were they attempting to negate disappointment[64] and ensure appointment?

The Bible describes angels—at least of the archangel variety—as difficult to distinguish from male human beings. So it's incredibly interesting that our pictorial images of angels are winged. Not many of the gods and goddesses of the ancient world were winged—but Lilith, Anat and Kairos were.

Joab never forgave Abner for spearing his brother. Perhaps he saw it as his duty as the kinsman-redeemer, the avenger of blood, to exact retribution for the killing. Abner eventually switched sides, supporting David rather than Ish-bosheth—and he joined David at Hebron, where he should have been safe from Joab. Hebron was, after all, a city of refuge. But David sent him away—in peace—and Joab, on discovering that had happened and having serious misgivings about Abner's change of allegiance, sent a message purporting to come from David. On luring Abner back, Joab then stabbed him to death in the gateway—before, of course, he could cross the threshold and come under the covenantal protection of the city.

David proclaimed his innocence in this murder but he never forgave Joab for arranging it. As he lay dying, it was one of two reasons he gave to Solomon for ensuring Joab was executed. The reward for Joab's loyalty—at times, obsessive and ruthless loyalty—was a death sentence. Joab fled to the Tabernacle and took hold of the horns of the altar—and there he was killed. It's unclear whether this was the Tabernacle erected by David to house the Ark of the Covenant or the Tabernacle of Moses that was still at Gibeon.

Either way, we see here an example of dispossession as not simply a loss of reward but as an inversion of it. This is a feature of a spiritualism, even into this postmodern age, that adheres to the principles of ancient Egyptian religion: upside-down, inside-out, back-to-front. When Anat has rights to empower this in our lives, our prayers will be answered in reverse. We won't get what we ask for from God—we'll get the opposite. Jesus becomes a danger, rather than a source of safety. He becomes a hazard, rather than a haven. In response to prayer, His answer is uncertainty, rather than peace; risk, rather than refuge; exposure, rather than covering; condemnation, rather than blessing; peril, rather than a way of escape.

As Arthur Burk says, Jesus is a liability rather than an asset when Egyptian spiritualism[65] is, for whatever reason, a significant force in our lives. That's not particularly evident in David's life but it plays a huge role in the kingship of Solomon.

In the latter years of David's reign, a three-year drought ravaged the land, so he inquired of the Lord as to the reason. Now drought and searing heat are usually a function of the spirit Resheph.[66] However, Resheph is worshipped together with Anat, so she soon makes her way into the picture. The spiritual legal rights behind the famine were not initially obvious to David, but God answered his inquiry with the revelation:

> *'It is on account of Saul and his blood-stained house; it is because he put the Gibeonites to death.'*
>
> 2 Samuel 21:1 NIV

Now did David inquire further of God? Did he ask how to make reparations? No, unfortunately, he inquired of the survivors of the Gibeonite massacre. And, as a result, he got himself into the most horrific of double-binds. Naturally, that made the situation far worse.

Anat's got a nice corner of the market when it comes to double-binds. Especially the ones that involve trust of God. To be able to get out of a double-bind, we need to be able to trust God. But all too often that's exactly why we're in the bind—because we can't bring ourselves to trust God, even though that's the only way out.

There are two kinds of double-binds; those that are:

- externally imposed
- internally created

The first kind are a strategy of dispossession promoted by Anat, while the second kind are a tactic of Rachab, the spirit of wasting. Of course, unless we resist the external imposition it can slide into an internal agreement.

People who cannot process shame and have fallen into narcissism are influenced by Lilith to try to impose double-binds on others. If they can succeed, then their victims will always be wrong while they are always right. And it would never dawn on those who see themselves as always right that they need to repent. Also, as we've noted, forgiveness has no meaning when it is offered to them. How could it? Forgiveness implies they did something wrong, but they've convinced themselves they were absolutely and totally in the right.

Now, by going to the Gibeonites to learn what they wanted in order to bless the Lord's inheritance,

David wound up breaking several covenants along with a specific oath. It turned out that they wanted vengeance—pure and simple. They wanted to take the lives of Saul's descendants. That's what they told David. What they failed to mention was that they wanted to defile the entire nation in the process. Their plan was diabolically cunning.

Over the intervening passage of years since the massacre, the remaining Gibeonites had cultivated a murderous hatred for the Israelites. They detested Saul but David wasn't exempt either. So when he came to them asking what they wanted in return for their blessing, they put it to him straight. They wanted his royal permission to sacrifice seven members of Saul's family.

At this point David should have taken a deep breath, gone outside to the Tabernacle to ask God's advice, then told the Gibeonites to make a second choice. He should have informed them he had a covenant with Saul that was not annulled by his death, likewise a covenant with Jonathan, also not annulled by his death, plus a covenant with Michal—Saul's daughter and, incidentally, David's wife. In addition to these covenants of defence that extended to the children and grandchildren of Saul, David had also sworn a specific oath when Saul had said:

> *So now swear to me by the Lord that you will not cut off my descendants after me and*

that you will not destroy my name from my father's household.

1 Samuel 24:21 NASB

David should have resisted the request of the Gibeonites and told them to *pick something else*. He should have informed them that he couldn't fix Saul's violation of the covenant with their people by, in turn, violating not just one but several covenants of his own with the family of Saul. Two wrongs don't make a right. That's the way he should have tackled the double-bind presented to him.

But he didn't. He was desperate to end the famine. In addition, he must have been seriously tempted by the political security that granting the request would bring. All of Saul's heirs—all the potential rivals to the throne from the previous king's line, every last one of them with the exception of Jonathan's son Mephibosheth,[67] who was disabled and therefore no threat—would be eliminated once and for all.

And so the Gibeonite trap was sprung. Now these Canaanites were servants to the Levites who ministered in the Tabernacle. They'd had centuries to learn the ways of Yahweh. Consequently, they knew how to maximise a show of contempt for Him.

Executing seven men of Saul's family, they *'exposed their bodies on a hill before the Lord,'*[68] right at the beginning of the barley harvest—that is, at Passover. In other words, at the most sacred time of year, human sacrifice was carried out. Instead of burying the bodies the same day, as honour of the dead required, they staked them out, allowing them to rot on the hill where the Tabernacle was situated. David didn't intervene. Everyone coming to the Tabernacle to celebrate Passover would have had a full view of this grisly spectacle. The Gibeonites notched up the existing defilement on the land, layer upon layer, to the highest degree.

David's offering to them didn't end the drought, it prolonged it. If Joab hadn't been right to agree to the game at the Pool of Gibeon that resulted in the sacrifice of twelve pairs of young men, then David wasn't right to sacrifice another seven in the same place. This was David's chance to show himself different from Joab and make a better choice—the circumstances are different but the spiritual set-up is the same: an offering to the spiritual powers of Gibeon, 'ha'elohim', who cannot possibly be Yahweh because He never asks for human sacrifice. In fact, He expressly forbade it and ordered redemption instead.

David had been tested and found wanting. He didn't keep his oaths when the going got tough and it was expedient not to. He'd promised Saul he would not cut off his descendants but he didn't keep that pledge. Perhaps he justified his actions with the thought, 'I'm not killing them; the Gibeonites are.' But that's a specious rationalisation.

Rizpah, Saul's concubine, was the one who changed the course of events. In deep mourning, she went to the hill of killing and, spreading out sackcloth, she drove away carrion birds during the day and wild animals at night. She assiduously protected the bodies that should have been buried the day they'd died.

In political terms, this was a public relations disaster for David. Anyone going to the Tabernacle at Gibeon to pray for the end of the drought could hardly have missed the lonely figure of Rizpah as, for months, she kept her harrowing vigil. From spring until autumn, she guarded the bodies, finally awakening David's conscience to the horrific dishonour he'd meted out to her family and the nation. Or perhaps it was her loyalty that guilted him into action.

David finally decided to rectify the situation by giving due dignity to Saul as well as to Jonathan and also to those men slain by the Gibeonites. Gathering all their bones—some from the other side of the Jordan—he ordered that they be interred in the family tomb. And it was at *that* point, not before, when some measure of honour was returned to the family, that God at last answered prayer on behalf of the land.

In this story we see an alliance between the threshold guardians. We see the double-bind influenced by Lilith as well as her signature style—spearing and staking; we see the dishonour that enables retaliation by Leviathan; we see Ziz behind David's forgetting to ask the Lord's advice; we see the abuse and defilement that is pushed by Belial; we see the selection of 'scapegoats' like those offered to Azazel; we see the pressure exerted by Python on David to make a decision that will bring an end to the drought and we also see the multiple levels of waste that Rachab perpetuates. All the threshold spirits are active in this story.

It's interesting to note that, in later life, David became afraid to go to Gibeon.

> *The tabernacle of the Lord, which Moses had made in the wilderness, and the altar of burnt offering were at that time on the high place at Gibeon. But David could not go before it to inquire of God, because he was afraid of the sword of the angel of the Lord.*
>
> 1 Chronicles 21:29–30 NIV

Things had changed drastically with David the giant-killer. He no longer had a deep and abiding sense of God's favour. I previously mentioned that David's loyalty to Yahweh wavered, when I was commenting on the ebb and flow of Saul's faithfulness to the Lord. At that point, you may not have believed me. But here we learn that, like Adam anxiously hiding from God, David is apprehensive and is staying right away from God's presence. The sweet psalmist of Israel who'd known the deep peace and companionship of God in times of trouble is terrified of the One who'd restored his soul.

Was the ultimate cause of his fear the double-bind the Gibeonites persuaded him to accept? Double-binds, after all, enable us to conceal from ourselves our lack of trust in God. And, in addition, they hide the shame of this lack of trust from us. The shame blooms into narcissism and self-righteousness—telling us we don't need to repent, we haven't done anything wrong. So we don't go to God.

Yet God pursues us. David couldn't go to Gibeon because he was afraid of the sword of the angel of the Lord. So God sent the angel with the sword to him.

> *David looked up and saw the angel of the Lord standing between heaven and earth, with a drawn sword in his hand extended over Jerusalem.*
>
> 1 Chronicles 21:16 NIV

David was a man of war. It seems, in the end, that was the only language he understood. Like those who come to be so reliant on God's grace they abuse it, David had to see God's favour withdrawn and experience the nakedness of His judgment before he could repent.

Those chroniclers who recorded the life of David worked exceptionally hard at impression management. They tell us David inquired of God about the cause of the famine, leaving us with the feeling that all that followed thereafter was stamped with divine approval. Of course, they don't actually say that, but that's the way they channel our thoughts.

When it comes to dubious actions, it's unwise to assume God's commendation unless the text explicitly says so. And it had better specify 'Yahweh' as the one giving the nod, otherwise we can't be sure there's not fallen angelic powers influencing events. God's reactions are, in fact, rarely found in the bare and basic outlines of history presented in the Hebrew section of Scripture.

His commentary on the past is always found in the life of Jesus.

That's where we should look. That's where any mending, if it is needed, will take place. Such repair work is what Irenaeus in the second century described as 'recapitulation'—a summing up of all things in Jesus' work of redemption.[69] There is a symmetry to salvation history and when we see Jesus repairing the past, then we know sin was involved—despite all the efforts of the chroniclers to spin the story so that the hero's halo never slips.

The interaction between David and the Gibeonites that resulted in the death of the sons of Saul mirrors that of Pilate and the chief priests that resulted in the death of Jesus. Both tragedies involved:

- events at Passover
- scapegoating innocent victims of the royal line
- spearing
- exposure of the victim on a hill outside the Tabernacle/Temple so that crowds celebrating a major festival would view the execution
- the one handing over the victim to the executioners wiping his hands of the situation
- a woman attending to the deceased after death and seeking to honour them
- people asking permission from a ruler in Jerusalem for the right to put another person to death. The Gibeonites said to David, *'It's not for us to execute anyone in Israel,'* (2 Samuel 21:4 ISV) and the chief priests said to Pilate, *'We are not permitted to execute anyone.'* (John 18:31 BSB)

David is not blameless in handing over the sons of Saul to the Gibeonites. He's just like Pilate. The parallel also indicates that the chief priests who condemned Jesus had the same contempt for God that the Gibeonites had. The chief priests, for all their pretensions, were no better than the despised labourers, those hewers of wood and drawers of water who served the Levites of old. Significantly Jesus is not compared to David in this recapitulation but to the sons of Saul. In the summing up of the Lord's work of redemption, that's what the equation says.

David's complicity with the ancient gods of Canaan went far beyond this terrible trade with the Gibeonites when he asks *them* what they want to lift the curse and bless the land, rather than ask God what is needed. He bought a threshing floor from the Jebusite king as a place for an altar—and eventually the site of the Temple. In Canaanite religion, this was a portal to their gods, a place of divination, where doom and judgment was pronounced, where marriages were celebrated, where wars were declared: all the sorts of things that needed a deity's oversight.

Not only was this site in Jerusalem utterly defiled and therefore a totally questionable choice, it's quite probable this is an example of dispossession on David's part. Not the Temple site itself—for which he paid Araunah handsomely—but the actual city. Jerusalem was in the tribal allotment of Benjamin, not Judah. Conquest didn't confer the right of possession in ancient Israel, since the tribes were meant to help each other in war. A woman was expected to marry inside her own clan so that, if her father had no sons, then her inheritance wouldn't pass outside the tribe and diminish its holdings.

When David conquered Jerusalem, he should have given over its stewardship to the leaders of the tribe of Benjamin. But that would have been to hand it over to the sons of Saul. You know, the ones he was supposed to treat kindly for the sake of his covenant with Jonathan. No doubt there were some excellent political reasons for keeping it and for moving his capital from Hebron to Jerusalem, but the underlying tones of dispossession are strong. He'd taken a city belonging to the inheritance of Benjamin and appropriated it for himself. Then he set about bringing the Ark of the Covenant there, and still later planned to bring the Tabernacle there by building a Temple to house it.

God quickly pointed out to David, asking him through the prophet Nathan if in all the centuries when a tent was the seat of His presence:

> *'Did I say a word to anyone from the tribes of Israel... "Why have you not built Me a house of cedar?"'*
>
> 2 Samuel 7:7 WEB

A Temple enhances David's glory, not God's. A Temple enhances David's political power, not God's. A Temple enhances David's prestige among the nations, not God's.

The Temple was not God's idea. Neither was the kingship, for that matter. But for the sake of His relationship with His people, God's Spirit descended to bless both anyway.

There is no one righteous; no, not one.

Romans 3:10 WEB

We know this truth, but we consider David only ever slipped up once and that the likes of Abraham, Joseph, Elijah and Paul deserve their pedestals anyway. Sometimes the sin in their lives is hidden by translations that minimise the gravity of their actions, sometimes preachers gloss over the wrongdoing as irrelevant to the thrust of their teaching topic, sometimes in our own reading we rationalise what's happening because there must be a good reason for the hero to behave so atrociously and sometimes—and these are the worst—we find commentators and scholars justifying the transgressions of the architects of our faith as right and good and proper and worthy of emulating.

We make exceptions to the 'no one is righteous' rule and think of many biblical figures as filling the blameless category when their offences against God and others are on clear display. Their stories are recorded for us, not so that we can slavishly mimic them but so that we, in the strength and the power of the Spirit of Jesus, can avoid the same mistakes. We are not called to copy their errors but to learn from them and do better.

In 1972, the Chinese Premier Zhou Enlai was asked by Henry Kissinger what he considered the impact of the French Revolution of 1789 was. 'Too early to say,' Zhou Enlai replied.

Probably right. Scripture, however, records the long-term effects of many ill-advised decisions and actions. In today's world, the conflict in the Middle East goes right back to Abraham and his toleration of abuse. It presents us the clear-cut message: 'Don't stand by and do nothing when people are being mistreated.'

We also see the long-term effects of Joseph's actions in the pages of Scripture and once again we have in front of us an unequivocal message: 'Dispossession will come back to bite your descendants.'

In Elijah's life, we are about to see the long-term effects of procrastination. Once again, there's a plain and unambiguous message: 'You can prevent a war by taking action a generation before it starts.'

When we ignore the failings of these great men of God—and, make no mistake, for all their weaknesses, they were indeed great, but *not* good or righteous—we deny human nature and reframe our heroes as, not merely godly, but effectively god-like. It's one of the oldest cultural impulses to deify our leaders. The ancient Egyptians did it with their god-kings, the Romans did it by divinising their emperors, the peoples of northern Europe euhemerised their rulers and the finest of their warriors, elevating them to godhood.

But the Hebrews didn't. Even as the scribes cranked up the celebrity status of the patriarchs and prophets, kings and judges, it was only to show us the heights from which they fell. The chroniclers might have engaged in impression management, but still they never let their biographies suppress the misdeeds, character flaws and failures of their subjects.

We, however, try to pretend those aspects of complicity with the realm of death, darkness and Sheol simply don't exist. And that's why we have such a hard time recognising Lilith and Anat in our lives—because we can't recognise that complicity even when it's plainly documented for us in the pages of Scripture.

I'm going to skip over Solomon, even though Scripture repeatedly describes him in the same language as the pharaoh of the Exodus. Solomon oppressed the Israelites, press-ganged them into slave labour and forced them to build storage cities and monuments. He married Pharoah's daughter but even that is a parallel since Rameses married several of his own daughters.

In a huge story twist the deliverer, like Moses, was under a similar death threat because of the king's anger, yet fled to—no, not Midian, not Gath—but Egypt. And then in yet another massive twist, this deliverer on his return from Egypt freed the people from the tormenting burden of servitude but, instead of bringing them back to God, encouraged them towards idol worship by using golden calves to represent Yahweh. However, Solomon slipped into a different kind of syncretism. He turned his back on the Lord and worshipped Moloch and other deities favoured by his foreign wives. His temple for Yahweh was just one of several.

David's utter ruthlessness[70] wasn't the only flaw in his character passed down to Solomon: so was his late-life shift in covenantal loyalty away from the Lord. Joseph dispossessed a people foreign to himself; Solomon dispossessed his own people. His son Rehoboam lost the kingdom because he was unwise enough to invite retaliation by announcing during his coronation week:

> *'My father scourged you with whips; I will scourge you with scorpions.'*
>
> 1 Kings 12:11 NIV

Rehoboam was responsible for tearing David's legacy apart. One tribe followed him and ten followed Jeroboam, that Moses-like deliverer who'd fled to Egypt and escaped Solomon. Jeroboam became the first ruler of the northern kingdom—eventually to be called the 'Kingdom of Israel' or, alternatively, 'Samaria' after the hill purchased by Omri, its sixth king, for his capital.

Omri's son, Ahab, married Jezebel in a political alliance with Tyre. With her arrival on the scene, the goddess Anat moved out of the background and onto centre stage once again. Jezebel's name comes from the liturgy involving the return of Baal-Hadad from the underworld. In the epic Baal Cycle, Anat's brother Hadad has died and she, as his fanatically loyal sister, spends the resulting seven years of drought looking for him. As she wanders from place to place, she calls, 'Where is the prince?' This cry of Anat's was used by the worshippers of Baal in their annual celebration of his return to life. They would stand outside a cave symbolising the underworld at the end of winter and call repeatedly: 'Where is the lord?' 'Where is the prince?' These ritual liturgically-charged words became the name *Jezebel*.

Queen Jezebel's devotion to Anat enables a resounding victory by the followers of Yahweh to be flipped over into a centuries-long defeat. It all happened after Elijah confronted the prophets of Baal and Asherah on Mount Carmel. There he'd demonstrated the worthlessness of the worship offered to them as well as their powerlessness to end the drought gripping the land.

Now it's important to understand the backstory to this momentous triumph. In his dramatic opening appearance, Elijah declares to King Ahab of Samaria that no rain is going to fall in the land until he—Elijah—says so. Then he disappears for three years, hiding out first in the Brook Cherith and then later in the coastal town of Zarephath, famous for its glass-blowers and metal-workers.[71]

Samaria is a dustbowl by the time Elijah returns. He initially meets up with Obadiah, the steward of

Ahab's palace, who is looking for pasture for the king's horses. Jezebel had embarked on a spree of murder, killing any prophets of the Lord she could find. However Obadiah, a loyal follower of Yahweh, had risked his own life to protect and provision one hundred of them. They are sheltered, hidden away in two caves.

This revelation of Obadiah's is immensely significant. He's the underrated legend in the story. Elijah hasn't faced the daily tension of providing food for others—instead he's been provided for, first by ravens, then by a widow. Nor has he faced the moment-by-moment prospect of betrayal and execution that comes with palace intrigue—instead he's been protected, first on the far side of the Jordan at the Brook Cherith, and later at Zarephath.

Obadiah's words provide the key to unlocking Elijah's failure. Three times—once at Mount Carmel and twice at Mount Horeb—Elijah declares he's the only prophet of God left. But, as Obadiah has indicated, there are a hundred more. We learn of several of these prophets in later chapters—solitary men who advise and often confront Ahab about his actions in the wars with Aram. Three of these prophets are anonymous,[72] but two are named—Michaiah, who predicts Ahab's death if he does not desist from battle and, of course, Elisha.

Now when Elijah met Ahab, he asked him to arrange for a contest between himself and the prophets of

Baal and Asherah. Although Scripture does not say so, it's clear that the Baal in question is Baal-Hadad, the storm-god and lightning-wielder, king of the Canaanite pantheon. Elijah had challenged his power by saying no rain would fall on the land until his say-so; now, three years on, this climatic showdown is to prove that, when rain comes, it's not because Hadad has finally answered the prayers of his supplicants.

The prophets of Baal-Hadad call on him all day long without answer. Elijah's turn finally comes, and he erects an altar of rough stones, drowns the wood and the sacrificial offering in water, then calls down fire from heaven. God answers by consuming everything on the pyre, including the water.

Following this, the prophets of Baal are killed, and a stormcloud rises from the sea, bringing a deluge of rain. It's what happens next that's all important to understanding Elijah's downfall. The next day, he receives a death threat from Jezebel. She's livid that the prophets of Baal have been killed and so sends a messenger to Elijah, saying:

> *'May the gods deal with me, be it ever so severely, if by this time tomorrow I do not make your life like that of one of them.'*

> 1 Kings 19:2 NIV

Elijah flees in panic. But why? He wasn't afraid, after all, to face 450 prophets of Baal and 400 prophets of Asherah. They're gone. He's got support: Obadiah's on side, the hundred prophets from the caves will back him up, and the populace will also be behind him now that drenching rain has arrived. Yet, he's so terrified by Jezebel's threat, he runs, taking with him a servant he seems to have suddenly acquired. What is in that threat that so unnerves him? Who are *'the gods'* Jezebel summoned?

Now remember she's named for the repetitious cry of Anat as she searches for Baal-Hadad. And remember that Anat is the obsessively loyal sister of Baal-Hadad and the daughter of the goddess Asherah—whose prophets Elijah has just slain. Jezebel was invoking Anat, along with the so-called 'young lions'—Hadad's brothers and Asherah's sons. 69 of them dwelt in palaces on Mount Hermon.

Now Elijah wasn't afraid of Baal-Hadad or Asherah, or for that matter, Leviathan, since on the way to and from Zarephath he'd crossed Leviathan's territory—the river Litani.[73] But clearly the thought of Anat was a different story. He can hardly be blamed for being utterly terrified. Anat was famously so fiercely protective of her favourite brother she hunted down the lord of Death who was, by the way, another of her brothers. She butchered Death for refusing to reveal Hadad's whereabouts in the underworld. Anat gloried in gore and wore the heads of her enemies on her belt. She slaughtered several of her brothers to protect her favourite, Hadad, and to advance his bid for the high throne above all other claimants.

Is it any wonder Elijah panicked? When he did so, however, a critical opportunity was lost.

Now Anat's name is derived from 'anah', *answer, testify, chant, sing, announce*. It is related to words for *poor, humble, meek, afflicted, downtrodden, defiled*. Also derived from 'anah' is 'eth', *time, appointed time, due season*. Anat's name relates to *appointed time* through the mutual link, 'anah'.

In Elijah's story, the appointed time had come to take down the government of Samaria. The first stage had been set with the removal of the prophets of Baal and Asherah. But Elijah was so afraid of Anat, he fled rather than trust in God's protection.

Elijah's assignment was to bring Samaria back to God. Had he seized the moment, then his mission would not have had to be completed by Jesus in a later age. History would have been so different. It was not God's will for Samaria to be overrun by the Arameans and later the Assyrians and for the tribes of Israel to be scattered. We can see this by the lengths God went to in trying to prevent those disasters. We can actually realise what would have happened because Jesus, as the Finisher of faith, completed the tasks the prophets had abandoned.

Elijah got as far as Beersheba, a six-day run from Samaria, before dismissing his servant. He was heading south—precisely the opposite direction to the stronghold of the 'young lions' on Mount Hermon. He was ensuring he was as far as possible from Anat and her brothers. His terror had abated but he'd fallen into a fit of depression. He'd tossed in the towel on his calling and he wanted to die.

Exhausted, he fell asleep under a broom tree and, on waking, he discovered that an angel had provided a breakfast of bread baked on hot coals. There's only one other breakfast of bread baked on hot coals mentioned in Scripture and it also occurs when God's chosen man has just thrown away his calling. Based on the second incident, on the shore of the Sea of Galilee after Jesus' resurrection, we can see that Elijah was not given the food of angels to keep on running, but to fortify him to turn back to the task at hand.

It was a crucial time. There was a power vacuum back in Samaria that needed to be filled by Yahweh's appointees, not by Jezebel's. The one hundred prophets could have come out of hiding and filled those positions of governmental advisors, bringing the nation back to God. But the opportunity for regime change was on the cusp of being lost. By the time Elijah had travelled another forty days down to Mount Horeb in the Sinai Desert, it was far too late. The prophets of Baal were back, fully restored to power as we see in the story of Michaiah—the lone voice speaking against four hundred hawks of war who were encouraging Ahab to go into battle. On that occasion, God had determined that the appointed time for Ahab's removal would no longer be delayed—and it's not a coincidence that the prophecy is delivered by Michaiah, the opponent of Ahab, rather than Elijah, his supporter.

Perhaps it seems shocking to label Elijah that way.

But consider Ahab's reluctant response to the king of Judah who asks if there's a prophet of Yahweh to consult:

> *'There is still one prophet through whom we can inquire of the Lord, but I hate him because he never prophesies anything good about me, but always bad.'*
>
> 1 Kings 22:8 NIV

Now what Ahab said next is one of those sudden twists that should come as a shocking surprise. He continues:

> *'He is Micaiah son of Imlah.'*

This is completely unexpected. He should be naming Elijah. After all, Elijah was still alive. Ahab implied here that he did not consider Elijah to be a prophet of Yahweh. This is a devastating judgment.

But when we look back at Elijah's inaction we realise Ahab had a point. Elijah was unwilling to be the agent of governmental change. His fear of the powers behind Jezebel outweighed his fear of God. Moreover, by default, he supported Ahab—refusing to anoint

Jehu as king even when the opportunity presented itself, and despite the fact he knew Jehu was chosen by God.

Now Elijah was not entirely wrong in supporting Ahab—at least to begin with. He was very wrong to continue once God had directed him to anoint Jehu as king.

Still, Ahab had inherited Joseph's mantle—the one that had gone through the hands of Sheerah, Joshua and Deborah and that carried with it the mandate to reverse dispossession and bring down full inheritance. There are several parallels between Joseph and Ahab:

- They both had fathers-in-law who were priests of a sun-god.
- They both had property in Samaria—Joseph was eventually buried, as he requested, at Shechem, the original capital of Samaria. Ahab's palace was on the hill of Samaria.
- They both lived during a time of famine and drought—Joseph prepared for it while Ahab blamed Elijah for it.

God's will for Ahab was to be the Joseph of his age and save his people from starvation. He should have built storehouses like Joseph, instead he built a palace of pearl. Had Elijah turned back after the breakfast delivered by the angel, Ahab's councillors and advisors would have been those hundred prophets of Yahweh hidden by Obadiah. Had that godly government happened, and the dispossession of Naboth been averted, then Elijah may never have even known that God's backup plan was Jehu. But once he'd fled as far as Horeb, the countdown began.

Still, Anat, the spirit of appointed time, doesn't want to see the Lord's candidates achieve their destiny on His designated day. Instead she strives to push the appointed time so far out it will occur beyond our lifespan. Elijah's fear of this goddess brought him into complicity with her. He missed opportunity after opportunity to obey God and change the government.

On reaching Mount Horeb, God asked Elijah what he was doing there. Elijah answered that he was the only prophet left, that the people had deserted God and that his life was in danger. Throughout his answer, he implies that he alone has been faithful to the commands of God. Ironic, since he was not only demonstrating his faithlessness and lack of trust in God at that point, he was about to double-bind himself into disloyalty and defiance.

God tried to shake Elijah out of his forgetfulness and feeling of rejection with an earthquake, wind and fire. And a silence—usually translated as a *'still, small voice'.* Then God asked him again what he was doing at Horeb. His answer was exactly the same. Nothing had changed. Elijah was stuck in trauma. God's question—designed to bring him to an acknowledgement of the truth, as well as recognition of shame—made no difference.

Normally, when commentators address Elijah's emotional condition, they name depression. However, I believe that his depression is a symptom, not the cause. Shame is a master emotion[74] and it can lie behind feelings of rejection, anger, anxiety and depression. I further believe that Elijah's speech to God indicates the depth of his shame—he's covered himself in self-righteousness at the expense of truth.

> *I have been very zealous for the Lord... The Israelites have rejected Your covenant, torn down Your altars, and put Your prophets to death... I am the only one left.*
>
> 1 Kings 19:14 NIV

These are half-truths. The people had just repented and 7000 had always remained loyal. Ultimately Elijah wouldn't be helped. He'd reached the limit of his trust in God and was trapped by his own fear.

So God gave him a way out. He basically told Elijah he could retire. There were just three matters that needed his attention first—anoint Jehu as king of Israel in place of Ahab, anoint Hazael as king of Aram in place of Ben-Hadad, and anoint Elisha as his own successor. All very safe tasks. He could avoid Jezebel completely. Elijah didn't need to cross the Jordan River to fulfil any of them; he just needed to travel the King's Highway up through the Transjordan and make three stops on the way.[75]

This was the divine Plan B: God was still intent on changing the government of Samaria. His alternative way of making that happen was through the anointing of Jehu. But God had an even more spectacular agenda hidden in His request to Elijah for the anointing of Hazael as king of Aram. But that agenda lay dormant and invisible for eight hundred years.

Jesus had to pass Elijah's mantle on to Simon Peter and set before him the task of completing Elijah's unfinished assignment. The true nature of that assignment only became clear when Peter received a message from the first century counterpart of the foreign army officer Hazael. *Vision of God* is the meaning of Hazael's name, and it's the vision of the foreign army officer Cornelius that entirely changed the direction of the early church. Cornelius was the first Gentile to become a Christian believer through the anointing of the Holy Spirit. We can therefore see that God's original plan was to bring the Gentiles into His kingdom through Hazael.[76]

But Elijah wasn't willing to cooperate and, as a result, the appointed time for the incoming of the Gentiles was delayed—by over eight *centuries!*

Elijah never anointed either Jehu or Hazael. It's not as if he didn't have the opportunity, at least in Jehu's case. They met up when Elijah prophesied against

Ahab over the death of Naboth and the confiscation of his vineyard.[77]

It's also unclear whether Elijah actually anointed Elisha.[78] It seems Elijah simply didn't want to retire as a prophet. So, he created a double-bind: while the tasks God had given him remained undone, his retirement was on hold. His lack of trust in God held him, as well as the nation, back. The wars with Aram would have been avoided if both Jehu and Hazael had come to know Yahweh.

Just as the rise of Assyria would have had an immensely different effect on world history if Elisha's protégé, Jonah, had preached about Yahweh to the people of Nineveh instead of merely pronouncing their doom.

Double-binds.

We saw several of them in David's life—the choice between keeping multiple covenants with the House of Saul or rescuing the wives and children who'd been abducted from Ziklag; and the choice between agreeing to the Gibeonite demands and, once again, keeping covenant. Now we see them in the life of Elijah—and also those of his successors, Elisha and Jonah.

Anat lurks in the background of these scenes. She's probably the Queen of Heaven mentioned by

Jeremiah. His hometown, Anathoth, a village just outside Jerusalem, was named after her.

Now admittedly many commentators consider the Queen of Heaven to be Asherah—however, in the city of Beit She'an on the Jordan river, that title was given to Anat. Just as Asherah was overtaken in popularity by Anat when the Israelite conquest began and the Canaanites needed a hard-hitting, take-no-prisoners battle-goddess, it seems more likely the people of Judah would appeal to a warrior Queen of Heaven when the Babylonian war machine was at their doorstep. Having abandoned God as covenant defender, Anat is the next logical choice. After all, she claimed to have defeated every major spiritual power.

In the Baal Cycle, her brother Hadad, the storm-god and cloud-rider, sent messengers to inform her he'd invented a wondrous new weapon—the lightning bolt. Anat, far from sharing his excitement, is puzzled by it. She wonders why he'd need such a device. Has a new enemy arisen? She's smashed all his known adversaries. Hasn't she slain Yam, the Sea? Hasn't she annihilated Nahar, the River? Hasn't she muzzled and thrashed Tannin, the sea monster? Hasn't she killed Lotan, the seven-headed coiling serpent?[79] Hasn't she snuffed out the darlings of the gods, Fire and Flame?[80] Hasn't she destroyed Mot, Death? Hasn't she been the one to smite the Flood, the notorious foe of Baal?[81]

By the time of Elijah, the light that shone so brightly when Sheerah and Joshua, and later Deborah and Barak, overcame Anat had dimmed almost entirely. The memory of God displaying His supremacy over her, subjecting her to a comprehensive defeat at appointed times in the past—the battle with the five kings or against Sisera—had been drowned in fear. The spirit of dispossession, disinheritance and life-draining had waxed triumphant.

Apparently Anat determined, after the crushing rout instigated by Deborah, that it wasn't happening again. *Ever.* Some people are surprised that spirits can learn from their mistakes, thinking they will always stick to the same strategy even when doesn't work. But generally they keep the same strategy because it *does* work.

It seems, from the way they cooperate, that Anat debriefed with Belial, the spirit of abuse, after the debacle in Deborah's days. Naturally, Belial's alter-ego, Kronos, the spirit of time, is aligned with Anat, the spirit of appointed time. Their alliance, already strong, cemented. And some resolutions were evidently put in place: anyone like Deborah was to be eliminated. If they somehow survived the attempts on their life, they were to be subjected to so much trauma that they would be terrified at even the thought of opposing her.

There were prophets before Deborah, but she was the first to shape history through a declaration of

God's word. Prophets ranged in the way they carried out their office. Abraham was a prophet because he could intercede for others, Aaron because he could be a spokesman, Miriam because she could sing praises. Only with Deborah does the current understanding of a prophet emerges. And it's only with Deborah that we see a defeat that wasn't overturned.

Now, of course, it may well have been overturned—but we aren't ever told that.

So, on the surface, it appears the main reverses suffered by Anat—the ones she wasn't able to turn back in a short period of time—happened because of Sheerah, Bithiah and Deborah. Notice the pattern. They're all women. And notably, as we shall see, in the stories where Jesus most strenuously opposes Anat, there's a woman too.

Lilith wants to dominate men, particularly male prophets. As Anat, she wants to subdue them and keep them in line through fear. On the other hand, Anat wants women gone. She's intent on making sure the success of Deborah never happens again. Anat and her allies have thousands of years of study behind them to know, often in the womb, if a girl has a gift of prophecy. She can throw everything at the child to ensure she never arises as a prophet and her voice is never activated.

This is not to say that men aren't a danger to Anat—they most definitely are. But they have less tendency to follow through. Joshua utterly defeated Anat but didn't take her power bases—Jerusalem and Beit She'an. Even beyond the cusp of victory, men tend to throw themselves backwards into defeat, as Elijah did. Women are much less likely to make truces with Anat than men are.

If we examine what happens with Elijah, we discover a fear that is shared by many of us:

- he was not afraid of Baal, Asherah or Leviathan—but he was mortally afraid of Anat
- he did not believe God could protect him against Anat—or else, he did not believe that God would protect him
- he believed that God was not as powerful as Anat—or at least, their powers rivalled each other's

As a consequence of these fears, Anat was able to dispossess Elijah of both his calling and the appointed time for the exercise of his calling. The result was:

- he wasted opportunities to fulfil the charge God had given him to anoint Jehu when they met
- he did not go, as instructed, to see Hazael and anoint him
- he left the commissioning of Jehu and Hazael undone for future generations of prophets to finish, but they followed his example and repeatedly delayed—Hazael was never anointed, despite the opportunity that

presented itself when he came to consult Elisha; and Jehu was only anointed after Hazael became king, as apparently a political backstop rather than obedience to God

- he role-modelled defiance of God for younger generations and this affected, in particular, Jonah—in the generation after Elisha
- he rejected divinely appointed times and allowed dispossession to result—if Jehu had been king of Samaria as God had directed, then Jezebel and Ahab would not have killed Naboth and his sons and appropriated their inheritance
- he did not make the effort to see or tell Gentile seekers like Hazael about Yahweh; and his attitude passed on to Elisha who, in turn, did not tell Naaman or Hazael about Yahweh either; and in the next generation of prophets, Jonah was so outraged by the prospect that God would have mercy on the Assyrians he would only deliver a message of doom, not mercy
- through his fear of Anat, he failed to oppose her claim to govern appointed time and so the appointed time for the incoming of the Gentiles to the Kingdom of God was delayed for over 800 years

We can't be sure, of course, but it's likely that—had Elijah been able to trust God would protect him—

that the wars with Aram would have been avoided. The rise of Assyria might have been averted. And even if that didn't happen, then the character of the Assyrian empire, by far the most feared and cruel of the ancient world, might have been radically changed.

Sure, these are the might-have-beens of history, not the verities, but we can see that this was what God wanted. His ideal will could only be achieved through Jesus. It's worth repeating: there is only one hero in Scripture and His name is Jesus.

It can feel depressing to realise that Elijah was meant to stop the wars with the Arameans, as was Elisha; Jonah was meant to stop the rise of Assyria, at least in the pitiless form in which it finally emerged; Hezekiah was meant to stop the rise of Babylon and their attendant war machine. See why it's a war for the soul of civilisation? If Anat can scare us enough so that we mute our own voices, if her allies can bully us sufficiently to neuter the power of our presence and the gift of Jesus that we carry, then the abuse and division we might be able nip in the bud will instead become a cankerous sore with generational repercussions. Instead of healing history, we harm it further.

The Hebrew people were called, right at their very foundation, to be a blessing to the nations—not merely by praying for them, as still happens today—but by introducing them to the King of the Universe.

And that's a major reason for the long, unconscionable history of antisemitism. Anat did a great job of making Elijah afraid and corralling him into a corner where he became tame and almost, but not quite, muted. It worked then, it works now. The technique is simple: create an existential threat, apply rulings to Israel that other nations are exempt from, make the Jewish people afraid and tempt them to hide their race. Then they'll not only shut up but the blessing they are meant to bring to the world will be minimised.

Jesus stands against all this. And He asks us to put on His armour and stand with Him. He puts out His nail-scarred hand so we can give Him the truce we've signed with Anat, along with permission to cancel the entire deal on the Cross. That's why He came. That's why Isaiah prophesied He would: because only God Himself could fix the defiled site that David had chosen and that Solomon had laid as a foundation.

At last, after all these discouraging episodes, some wonderfully good news! Isaiah has taken a serious look at Joshua's battleplan and figured out exactly what he did to bring to nothing Anat's claim to rule over appointed time. He analysed the detail and realised there's a way to ensure that the defeat of Anat is accomplished. And then, even better than working out how it could be done, Isaiah got the court of King Hezekiah and the leaders of Jerusalem to implement it. He took the theory and brought it to fruition. That means we can take his strategy, *adapt* it under God's guidance, and be victorious ourselves.

Notice I said *adapt* it. Don't forget that threshold spirits are hyper-intelligent beings. They learn from their defeats. If we use the same tactic over and over, expecting it to work every time, we will soon be disappointed: after all, we've really developed a formula rather than learned to rely on God. So many people adopt the strategy, biblically-based to be sure, of singing songs of worship in the face of the enemy. Perhaps we choose it because it's easier to implement than digging trenches, which is just as biblically-based.

This isn't to say that songs of worship are irrelevant: in fact, they are a vital weapon against Anat. The Septuagint—the Greek translation of the Hebrew Scriptures from about two centuries before the birth of Christ—translates the words of Isaiah associated with Lilith as *sirens*.[82] They're apt to be portrayed as mermaids but they are actually bird-human hybrids. They were made famous in Homer's epic poem, *The Odyssey*. Sirens are vampiric in nature, luring sailors to their deaths with the enchantment of song.

Our worship songs to God disrupt the songs of the enemy, perhaps even the communication band used by hostile powers. But this is not the same as defeating them. For that, we have to ask God what His strategy is.

That's obviously what Isaiah did. His insight is well-known. The words of the Sovereign Lord he relays to the besieged people of Jerusalem are:

> *Behold, I lay in Zion a stone for a foundation, a tried stone, a precious cornerstone, a sure foundation; whoever believes will not act hastily.*
>
> Isaiah 28:16 NKJV

This is quoted and requoted in the epistles as a reference to Jesus the Chief Cornerstone. But look at the implication: something is wrong with the foundation, something terribly amiss with the very beginning of Zion. The epistles of Peter and Paul reveal that this prophecy tells us that nothing less than Jesus Himself will suffice as a replacement. And that in turn tells us that God was not the original foundation.

In view of this essential wrongness in the foundation, the way this verse in translated into Greek and then quoted in Romans takes on deep significance:

> *Behold, I lay in Zion a stumbling stone and rock of offense, and whoever believes on Him will not be put to shame.*
>
> Romans 9:33 NKJV

When we perceive ourselves as wrong in the very core of our being, we experience shame. But here we discover that, when Jesus becomes our new Cornerstone, He will not allow us to be put to shame.

Now back in Isaiah, the prophet sandwiched this verse about the Cornerstone between two others that expose the problem besetting the rulers of Jerusalem. One of these is:

> *You have said, 'We have made a covenant with death, and with Sheol we have an agreement, when the overwhelming whip passes through it will not come to us, for we have made lies our refuge, and in falsehood we have taken shelter.'*
>
> Isaiah 28:15 ESV

In verse 17, on the other side of the sandwich, God says that hail will sweep away the refuge of lies—the false refuge—and a deluge will overwhelm the shelter—the hiding place. The word for *hiding place* implies that it contains a secret shrine for idols.

Our false refuges can cover an immensely wide spectrum, ranging from consolations as innocent as coffee or as destructive as pornography.[83] When we are thwarted—when the opportune time or position seems to have slipped past, when Anat has somehow elbowed us out and turned appointment into disappointment—then we all tend to seek comfort with a false refuge, not with God. Jesus is our last resort, not our first port of call.

Now I used to think a covenant with Death and an agreement with Sheol were the same. Partly because the word translated *agreement* was so hard to understand in context and, for years, I couldn't make sense of it. It's actually *seer*—a prophet gifted with sight, insight and vision into the spiritual realm. Finally I realised this is Anat's most diabolic strategy for disabling those who will pose the greatest threat—she lures those gifted as seers into trading with Sheol.

Now Sheol is sometimes translated *hell*, but that gives entirely the wrong impression. The *grave* is better, but it still doesn't have quite the right nuances. Sheol is *afterlife*, but not in the fire and brimstone category. Sheol is sometimes described as a person and sometimes a place but, as we've seen, so is Anat and so is Leviathan ('place' being furniture in his case).

And so are we.

Much of the information about Sheol in Scripture seems confused and contradictory, but one constant remains. In Sheol, the inhabitants are blind. Their greatest desire is to see. That's why a seer is so valuable a commodity. In exchange for sight, the seer is offered knowledge. That's the one thing Sheol has in abundance. So many people take their secrets and shame to the grave—thus inflicting iniquity on their descendants. The source of the repeated generational reaping in the lives of their children and grandchildren often remains hidden. The Holy Spirit can, of course, reveal it. But so can Sheol.

If seers are gaining knowledge from Sheol—and it's quite possible for them to be unaware of this—then their prophecies can be supernaturally accurate but nevertheless not coming from heaven. This is a significant reason why we are cautioned by Jesus to discern His followers by examining the Fruit, not the Gifts. Accuracy is no guarantee that the source of revelation is the Holy Spirit.

Necromancy is divination involving consulting the spirits of the dead. It's Lilith's occult specialty. The trading of sight for knowledge—the agreement with Sheol that involves an exchange of seer gifting for arcane knowledge—is primarily necromancy. It is divination, that is, foretelling the future. The means used is knowledge obtained from the grave. Prophecy, unlike divination, is not foretelling but forthtelling. For the Hebrews, it was an inspired ability to discern a pattern and make a prediction on that basis. That prediction was not normally set in cement or engraved in stone. It was living, flexible, organic—it was more often than not conditional and could be altered by the responses of those who received it. Consider, for example, the people of Nineveh who heard Jonah's prophecy of doom, *'Yet forty days and Nineveh will be destroyed,'* and who responded with repentance.

Divination, on the other hand, is an attempt to pronounce an inescapable fate.[84] So-called 'Christian clairvoyance' falls into this category. 'Christian clairvoyance'—knowledge about another person's life so private only that other person knows—is sometimes used as an evangelistic technique to open up a conversation with a person who might be resistant to the gospel. It's an abuse of the seer gifting.

Most believers unfortunately assume that, if a professing Christian starts to misuse a gift given to them by God, that He will automatically withdraw it. This is not the case.

> *The gifts and the calling of God are irrevocable.*
>
> Romans 11:29 ESV

Of course the gifts of God are never withdrawn. They would not be *gifts* otherwise. This is why we can see people of immense talent operating in an extraordinary level of spiritual gifting but leading a totally godless lifestyle behind the scenes. It's worth reminding ourselves yet again that Jesus told us we are to know one another by the fruit of our lives. *Fruit*, not gifts.

Speaking of the Fruit of the Spirit, let me foreshadow the flavour that overcomes Anat. If you've read any other books in this series, you'll be aware that the Fruit of the Spirit is an arsenal of weapons, designed to assist us in overcoming different threshold spirits. *Love* is best deployed against the spirit of Python; *joy* against the spirit of Ziz; *peace*, 'shalom', against the spirit of Leviathan; *self-control* against Azazel; and *goodness, kindness* and *faithfulness*, 'chesed', against Belial. In the case of Anat or Lilith, the most effective armament is *gentleness*. Not to be understood as niceness, tolerance, lenience or indulgence but as *strength under control, power regulated by authority.*

Authority is frequently misunderstood: it is the delegated right to uphold the Word and the will of God, not to make up our own rules as suits our purposes in the moment. We don't exercise true authority by manipulation, coercion or overriding the free will of another person. That's abuse and corruption and, if we insist on using our authority in that way, then we must take the inevitable consequences. They might take a decade or two to became apparent—God, in His mercy, makes them as slow-moving as a steamroller and, in His justice, makes them as crushing as a steamroller too. There is a singular problem with the belief that God gives us the authority to make up our own rules. It's quite simple: God will hold us to those very same rules. Unfortunately for us, He passionately detests hypocrisy.

For most of us, the effect of a prophecy that's bolstered by supernatural knowledge no one outside ourselves knows is so dazzling that it all too often causes us to simply accept the word as coming from God. When we buy in without question, we fail to exercise the discernment the Lord has given us.

> *A prophet or a diviner of dreams may arise among you, give you an omen or a miracle that takes place, and then he may tell you,*

> *'Let's follow other gods (whom you have not known) and let's serve them.' Even though the sign or portent comes to pass, you must not listen to the words of that prophet or that diviner of dreams. For the Lord your God is testing you, to make known whether or not you'll continue to love the Lord your God with all your heart and soul.*

Deuteronomy 13:1–3 ISV

Looks like it's easy to pick out a false prophet. As soon as they advocate following 'other gods', it's time to run. But no one is as blatant as that. No one is as obvious as: 'I've got a freshly baked loaf of the most scrumptious divinely-smelling consecrated bread and a group of us are going up to the park first thing in the morning to worship Tammuz at sunrise. There's gonna be a portal of power opening. Wanna come?'

It's much, much, much more subtle. It's commending someone on their coping mechanism, failing to call it out as a false refuge, thus reinforcing the power of the idol behind every source of consolation that usurps the place of Jesus. Sometimes it can be slightly more overt in leaving Jesus out of the picture. If I'd realised earlier in life that a consistent, regular choice to sideline Jesus was indicative of a truce with Anat, I'd have been able to counter it much more effectively. Mostly when I was aware of such situations, they left me speechless. I'd think, 'But you're such a good Christian. So much better than me.'

Sigh. Yes, it's so easy to forget that no one is good, except God alone.

Even now, twenty years after I first encountered the phenomenon of erasing Jesus allegedly in order to promote Jesus, it still takes me by surprise. But what I find even more surprising is that people invariably defend their actions. I've had to challenge an author who'd written an entire autobiographical series but never given a hint of her nationwide ministry in it or her devotion to Jesus; I've had to challenge men who regularly see signs and wonders come to pass through miraculous healings in the street but who never attribute the healing to Jesus; I've had to challenge a pastor who allowed a member of his staff to pray for others without ever involving Jesus as the mediator in the prayer. The pastor was a Baptist and the staff member's husband was a Buddhist—and that was why she had become uncomfortable about praying in the name of Jesus.

In every one of these cases—and in so many others where I've spoken to a group rather than individuals—the decision to push Jesus so far to the margin He was invisible has always been justified by: 'But people will know anyway.'

No, they don't. They simply don't. They have no idea. Maybe a hundred years ago, the assumption that people would know might just have been reasonable. But today it's not even remotely likely. By not mentioning Jesus, we fail to proclaim the good news. We also play a power game: we project the image of ourselves as the mediator of answered prayer, not Jesus.

Every treaty with Anat, every truce with Lilith, every agreement with Sheol contains a clause: 'This is just between you and me. We can leave Jesus out of this. Let's not make a big deal of the whole thing. Let's just quietly agree amongst ourselves.'

We see this aspect of the deal in the lives of the prophets. Once Elijah has been scared witless by the prospect of Anat hunting him down, he starts to leave Yahweh out of the picture. Not entirely, of course, but mostly. Similarly Elisha won't even see Naaman to start with, but will only send him instructions. Naaman becomes utterly and completely open to learning the ways of Yahweh once he's healed of leprosy, but all he gets is some turf to take home so he can worship the God of Israel on it. The people of Nineveh are similarly open to learning of Yahweh when Jonah pronounces a coming destruction but rather than rejoice in their repentance, Jonah is angered by God's mercy in response.

So what does Isaiah recommend when we want an annulment of our covenant with Death and our agreement with Sheol? Naturally, we have to repent of our false refuge and the worship of whatever idol we've installed in it, and we have to repent of mocking God.

> *Now stop your mocking, or your chains will become heavier; the Lord, the Lord Almighty, has told me of the destruction decreed against the whole land.*
>
> Isaiah 28:22 NIV

The Hebrew for *mock* is 'luts', rhyming with 'luz', the former name of Bethel. Luz probably meant *almond*, but it has overtones of *turning away, departing* and also *night*—understood as a turning away or a departure of light. It's therefore connected to Lilith whose name also derives from *night*. Even with a renaming, the city never really lost its association with Lilith—in later days, Anat-Bethel probably signifying 'Anat, consort of Bethel' is used as a threat in a treaty between Assyria and Tyre.[85] Although she is not mentioned in Scripture, just attested outside, we can detect her influence in the Egyptian-inspired golden calf erected at Bethel as well as the nickname given to it by the prophets: Beth-Aven, *house of evil.*

Did Isaiah actually intend with this wordplay around 'luts' to refer obliquely to Bethel? His allusions in this passage are so dense and intricate, I personally don't doubt he did.[86] The entire chapter is a masterpiece of poetry in the chiastic style—that is, it's mirror-symmetrical around a central verse, that famous one already quoted about the Lord laying a Cornerstone in Zion.

The beginning of the chapter repeatedly draws attention to a *wreath*, a *crown*, belonging to Ephraim.

Like the end of the chapter which features a threshing floor, it's about things that circle around and around. In fact, a crown that circled the entire head was rare in the Hebrew world. Kings were more likely to wear diadems than crowns. Even amongst the godlings and goddesses, full crowns were rare—though it will not be a surprise, I'm sure, to know that Anat had one.

In the first half of the chapter—the build-up to God laying a new Cornerstone—the problem is laid out. It's drunken pride, rampant injustice, covenanting with spiritual powers, and scoffing at God while stringing together pleasant and reassuring lines from His word. It's also false refuges of intoxicating drink and relentlessly positive propaganda to relieve anxiety and create a delusion of safety. The Assyrians have 185,000 troops over in the next valley but don't worry—we've taken out foolproof spiritual insurance and we've got a treaty with Death and truce with Sheol. In return for dispossession and for sight, they'll let us survive.

Now as soon as Isaiah starts to refer to God as the only true protector, he brings in allusions to one of the most underrated characters in Scripture: Ephraim's daughter, Sheerah. Isaiah has signalled 'Ephraim' right at the beginning of the chapter to clue us in to where this is going. Then he becomes more explicit.

> *In that day the Lord of hosts will be a crown of glory, and a diadem of beauty, to the remnant* ['shear', the same meaning as Sheerah] *of His*

people, and a spirit of justice to him who sits in judgment, and strength to those who turn back the battle at the gate ['shaerah'].

Isaiah 28:5-6 ESV

In verse 28, he refers to 'showrah'—probably meaning *rows*, and also to 'sheorah', *barley*, both puns on the name Sheerah.[87] Back in verse 23, he says, *'Give ear and listen,'* which is 'uzzen', part of the name of one of Sheerah's cities. But the sure reason this is not mere coincidence is the double reference to Sheerah's twin cities of Beth-Horon:

The Lord will rise up as He did at Mount Perazim, He will rouse Himself as in the Valley of Gibeon—to do His work, His strange work, and perform His task, His alien task.

Isaiah 28:21 NIV

Repeatedly mentioned throughout this chapter are violent hailstorms and torrential deluges that sweep all before them. They are the work of the Lord, says Isaiah. And though he doesn't mention them explicitly here in verse 21, they are to be understood in the battles that he is referring to. Mount Perazim refers to a pincer movement by the Philistines against Jerusalem in the time of David that was obliterated by an inland tsunami—reminiscent of that flash flood on the Kishon river in the time of Deborah. The fleeing Philistine battalions, unnerved by the sudden loss of an entire wing of their army, were pursued and were caught on the narrow ascent between Upper and Lower Beth-Horon.

Likewise, the Valley of Gibeon refers to another battle that culminated on the Ascent of Beth-Horon. This was Joshua's victory over the five Amorite kings—when he asked for the sun and moon to stand still, for time to be altered so that the campaign against the enemy could be finalised.

The twin cities of Beth-Horon were the first places built by a descendant of Abraham in the Promised Land. They are therefore *cornerstone* cities; they are the foundation of the nation—though they were never recognised as such. As the cornerstone, they are places of covenantal protection. Isaiah looks to them and points out that this is a place where miracles of divine defence against overwhelming odds happen. He could have mentioned Jonathan's attack on the Philistines at Michmash that also came to a conclusion on the same hillside. Unknown to him, in later times, a decisive battle by the Maccabees, as well as the total defeat of a prestigious Roman legion, would occur on this same spot.

Isaiah's message is this: there's a problem with the foundation at Zion. We'd be far better off with something like Beth-Horon. Nevertheless God can fix even the foundation. He'll go right back to the cornerstone, the very first building block to be laid and He'll start again and make it perfect. In the meantime, if you want God to come to your defence as He did in times past, then:

- repent of your false refuges
- toss out the idols you've hidden in them
- renounce your covenants with Death and Sheol
- cease playing around with God's Word
- stop mocking Him.

Then He'll annul those covenants and He'll deal with the retaliation that's due to come your way for daring to ask for them to be cancelled.

Now the rulers of Jerusalem that Isaiah denounced in such scathing terms must actually have listened. King Hezekiah had to be brought to the brink of death to get to that point, and he had to rise from his deathbed to take the message from the Rabshakeh, the Assyrian field commander—a message he was too ill to receive in person—and go to the Temple to plead for God to answer the affront to Himself and His people.

Isaiah relays back God's message of mercy, indicating that the king of Assyria will hear a rumour of an attack on his own land and return to it. But Sennacherib doesn't leave without sending a stern warning message and he doesn't take all his army. That huge force poised at the gates of Jerusalem stays in place. The siege hasn't lifted.

Hezekiah lays out the message before the Lord, asking for help. Told to make himself ready for death, he weeps and asks God to remember his faithfulness. Isaiah returns to him to tell him the Lord has seen and heard him and will extend his life. He is to ask for a sign. Now Hezekiah doesn't make the mistake his father Ahaz did of refusing to ask for a sign from God. Given the choice between the shadow of the sun moving forward on the stairway of Ahaz that served as a sundial and it going backward, he chooses backward: he asks for time to reverse.

So Isaiah called on the Lord, asking for the shadow to move ten steps backward. And it does. This is only the second time in Scripture that time is *explicitly* altered. Again it's in the middle of a war. As Isaiah had prophesied, God's intervention as covenant defender was just as spectacular as that time-freezing moment when Joshua called on the sun and moon to stand still. Just as hail—personally I think the word means *meteorite*, but let's not quibble—smashed the armies fleeing from Joshua, and in a later century the stars in their courses fought for Deborah and Barak against Sisera (meteorites again?), so the 185,000 Assyrian troops were dispatched by an angel overnight.

The people woke up to find the siege was over. The enemy were all dead. The miracle was so stupendous that news filtered through to the neighbouring nations. So the Babylonians—at that time an insignificant power on the world stage—sent envoys to Jerusalem to make inquiries about Hezekiah's return to health. Now clearly that was an excuse. The Babylonians had a centre of learning, a court of astronomers, astrologers, mathematicians and geometers who would become known as 'magi'. They'd have noticed a change in time—it wouldn't just affect their astronomical tables, it would affect their astrological charts. Rumour obviously reached them that it was about something that happened in Jerusalem.

So they came to see Hezekiah—and he showed them everything. He impressed them with all the treasures still left. The palace and the Temple were still magnificent, even though Hezekiah had stripped the gold from the Temple doors as the price of a temporary truce with the Assyrians.

Isaiah chastised him, prophesying that in time the Babylonians would return—as they did a century and a half later—and take everything they'd been shown. Yet Hezekiah apparently hadn't told the Babylonians about the greatest treasure of all—the only lasting one. He hadn't opened to them a knowledge of the God of Israel.

Like Elijah, Elisha and Jonah before him, he couldn't share Yahweh. Had Elijah, Elisha and Jonah made different choices, the wars with the Arameans and the Assyrians might never have eventuated. Had Hezekiah made a different choice, the Babylonian conquest might have been avoided. Here we see another moment when God tried to stop a war by bringing Israel as a light to the nations. Yet once again, when the opportunity presented itself, those in charge marred the chance.

Let's not involve Jesus—that's the non-negotiable clause in any truce with Anat. She promises us opportunity if we marginalise Him. She hints that appointment, rather than disappointment, is soon to come our way. But she uses 'soon' in heaven-speak: Jesus, after all, is the One for whom 'soon' is 2000 years and counting. And Jesus is the only One who can turn disappointment into appointment, not Anat.

Like the rulers of Jerusalem in the time of Hezekiah, we need to repent of our false refuges, and renounce our covenants with Death and Sheol. Then we can expect miracles of timing.

Prayer

Please do not even consider praying the following prayer unless you have dealt with, and been tested on, the known false refuges in your life and are committed to dealing with any the Holy Spirit may reveal as you journey with the Lord. How to deal with false refuges is detailed in the fourth book in this series, *Hidden in the Cleft*.

Note: this prayer is simply a prompt to start you off. Please don't use it as a formula but, under the guidance of the Holy Spirit, add to it or subtract from it as He leads. Because this prayer involves covenant annulment, it is best done with a witness. Say it aloud.

Gracious Lord and Heavenly Father,

I ask Jesus of Nazareth to be my mediator as I pray. I hold on to the fringe of His prayer shawl with my tiny seed of faith and I ask that He takes it and breathes His prayers over it so that it is given life to achieve all You want in me and through me.

Forgive me for the times I've chosen to follow some 'hero' other than Jesus. Forgive me for the times when I looked on the actions of the patriarchs, prophets and kings as pleasing to You and worthy of emulating, when they were so offensive in Your eyes. Forgive me for the times I casually called someone 'good' when I know that Jesus so clearly said, *'No one is good— except God alone.'* Forgive me for abusing Your grace by setting my sights lower when it comes to the calling You have placed before me and thinking I could achieve so much of it in my own strength. Truly, Lord, without You it is beyond my capability and You always intended it to be so. Help me to trust You so that I can step forward into that calling, but more importantly, into a deeper communion with You.

Lord, I speak out forgiveness to those in my bloodline and faithline who have abused and disinherited others. I speak forgiveness to Noah for cursing his grandson, Canaan, with slavery, I speak forgiveness to Sarah for her abuse and to Abraham for sending his son Ishmael away with less than that an honoured guest would receive, I speak forgiveness to Rebecca for facilitating a deception and splitting her family, I speak forgiveness to Jacob for stealing his brother's birthright, I speak forgiveness to Joseph for dispossessing the Egyptians and inventing forced resettlement and giving them no way of redress, I speak forgiveness to Moses for refusing to accept his God-given identity and name, I speak forgiveness to David for repeatedly breaking covenant with others, I speak forgiveness to Elijah for his procrastination and defiance of Your will.

Lord, I ask Jesus to empower my words of forgiveness through His cross to achieve the cleansing of my bloodline and faithline.

I recognise that the motivation behind all these sinful actions is a fear of lack and a distrust of You—that You cannot be relied upon to provide or to defend in times of trouble. That belief, Lord, is hidden deep in the foundation of my heart. It's there in my cornerstone and I cannot access it. Instead, I all too often deny it. I say I trust You. But, if I did, I wouldn't have paused here for so long. I'd be racing headlong into my calling as I follow Your footsteps.

I repent of cursing, enslaving, abusing, neglecting, deceiving, stealing, dispossessing, refusing covenant, breaking covenant, procrastinating, defying—all the negative things that have come down my faithline and bloodline, mixed with blessing and miracles of healing, provision and timing. Again I ask Jesus to empower my words of repentance and charge them with life through the power of His Cross so they can achieve the turnaround You desire.

Lord, I ask You to rebuke all the threshold spirits, but particularly Anat, casting them out, directing them to go to the place appointed for them. I ask that this is applied to them in all their guises and under whatever alias they are operating in my life. Further, I ask You, Father, to fulfil Your promise of annulling the covenant with Death and the agreement with Sheol. I ask that any other covenants I have with threshold spirits also be included.

Lord, please forgive me and my ancestors—both bloodline and faithline—for trading sight for knowledge with Sheol and for exchanging inheritance for survival with Death. I repent of these trading agreements and ask You to nullify them through the Blood and Cross of Jesus.

I renounce—I say *forever no* to—the covenant with Death and I ask Jesus to cancel it on His Cross. I renounce the agreement with Sheol and I ask Jesus to cancel it, once again, on His Cross. I ask Him also to forbid backlash against me for revoking these covenants with Death and the underworld. I thank Him for having already paid the price for all of this to happen, so that I may be free.

I renounce the false lights and light-bearers, I renounce the unholy light-bringers and lamp-lighters, I renounce the ungodly torch-bearers under whatever alias they assume: Anat, Athena, Neith, Minerva, Lilith, Astarte, Asthoreth, Isis, Ishtar, Lucifer or any other name. I ask for the false lights to be extinguished in my life and for only Jesus as the Light of the World to be my source of illumination. I renounce any complicity I have with them that might put me under the authority of the judges and rulers they decide should be the ones who determine my destiny. Only You, Lord, have that right.

Lord, I also ask that You remove from me, as the Temple of Your Holy Spirit, *anything*—a spirit, a spiritual deposit, a spiritual claim, patent, copyright, defilement, payload or anything else that Jesus cares to name on my behalf—that is not in accord with

Your design and desire for me. I ask that anything that results in a spirit being able to claim he or she is in me and I am in him or her be completely done away with, utterly removed, and the place cleansed by the Holy Spirit.

I also ask that I be placed securely in Jesus and He in me. That He be given to me as a Cornerstone to replace what I have from conception.

Where I have been in 'Egypt', in Sheol, and have taken on the spiritualism of that place, so that my prayers are answered back-to-front, upside-down, inside-out, always in reverse, I ask that You fight Anat and any of the other divinities of the land of dispossession on my behalf. I renounce the belief that my prayers will be answered in an inverse way. I ask that You annul any covenants with 'Egypt' that are additional to the ones already spoken of and that, once again, You forbid backlash for the cancellation of these covenants. I further ask that You sever any spiritual supply lines into or out of me that resource the battle against me or others.

Speak, Lord, Your favour over me and give life to all the words I have spoken and the decisions I have declared today.

> In the name of Jesus of Nazareth,
> the only truly *good* Man.
>
> Amen

3

Just Ask Me

The lion told me I must undress first... I was just going to say I couldn't undress because I hadn't any clothes on when I suddenly thought that dragons are snaky sorts of things and snakes can cast their skins... So I started scratching myself and my scales began coming off all over the place. And then I scratched a little deeper and... my whole skin started peeling off beautifully. I just stepped out of it... But just as I was going to put my feet in the water I looked down and saw that they were all hard and rough and wrinkled and scaly just as they had been before... So I scratched and tore again and this underskin peeled off beautifully and out I stepped... Well, exactly the same thing happened again. And I ... got off a third skin... But as soon as I looked at myself in the water I knew it had been no good.

Then the lion said... 'You will have to let me undress you.'

CS Lewis

The undragoning of Eustace in
The Voyage of the 'Dawn Treader'

THE COUNTER-ATTACK WAS not long in coming. The indigenous woman I wrote about previously was soon threatened with dispossession once again. Various relatives who wanted the land for their side of the family, rather than for the entire community, ganged up and decided to take the matter to a higher court. They were bullying and intimidating in their behaviour and made it clear they would attempt to get the verdict overturned.

The prayer team gathered again to pray with her, looking to Scripture to see what story corresponded to her circumstances. Now it was a family matter, so we focussed on those biblical stories where brother had dispossessed brother. Was the situation, we asked, like Jacob's theft of Esau's birthright? Or was it closer to Ishmael's loss of not just his birthright but his father's presence in order to ensure Isaac would inherit the rights of the firstborn? In fact, so that Isaac would inherit as if he were an only son.

We decided it was a bit of both scenarios but mostly the second. So this time our prayer in terms of faithline iniquity focussed on forgiveness for Abraham and Sarah. Consider: Sarah had engineered Ishmael's birth, treated him as her son until Isaac arrived, then demanded he be sent away because he was laughing. Did God punish her for doing *exactly* the same? Despite some translations saying Ishmael *mocked* Isaac, that's an interpretation: the words used for both *laughing* and *mocking* are exactly the same.

Sarah laughed at God—and He rebuked her. But her response to Ishmael's laughter is not to rebuke him but to drive him away. Now God did indeed tell Abraham to do as Sarah said, but that doesn't mean how they carried that out was right. To send Ishmael off with nothing more than what he and his mother could personally carry is callous. Abraham was an exceedingly wealthy man with herds of cattle, sheep, donkeys, camels, slaves—but not one is given to his son to transport either food and water for survival. Such an action is tantamount to a death sentence. And both Abraham and Sarah would have known that the chances of Ishmael's and Hagar's survival was slim. Sarah's attitude was vindictive and vicious—she had abused Hagar for years, but by the time Isaac was weaned she wanted her dead.

That's the secret desire behind all dispossession. It says: 'I want you dead so I can inherit.' It's not simple robbery. It's theft accompanied by murder in the heart. And that, according to Jesus, is equivalent to murder.

That's why I think God told Abraham to follow Sarah's directions: because her hatred had become so intense that, if Hagar and Ishmael weren't sent away, they'd be found dead. Make no mistake: Sarah was active in abuse, Abraham passive. God had warned them of the consequences nearly two decades previously. At that time, He'd codified the reaping—hundreds of years of mistreatment and slavery for their descendants as strangers in a foreign land, to begin in the fourth generation—into His first covenant with Abraham.

So, that's what we unpacked as we looked at this attempt by the family of this indigenous woman who were threatening to escalate the matter to a higher court. She went through the process, not only forgiving them, not only forgiving those males in her bloodline who'd been passive in the face of their wives' abuse of others, but also forgiving the faithline back to Abraham and Sarah. Then of course, the prayer team asked Jesus to empower these words of forgiveness.

A few days later, the group opposing her walked into a meeting and signed some documents that meant their threat of further legal action simply vaporised.

The life of Jesus is characterised by *recapitulation*. This is the term used by Irenaeus, the second-century bishop of Lyons. He'd been taught by Polycarp who, in turn, had been mentored by the apostle John. Recapitulation is the oldest theory of the atonement. By it, Irenaeus meant that Jesus had reenacted the events leading up to the Fall, but with a change in the storyline to correct Adam's sin.

Irenaeus borrowed the term *recapitulation* from the art of rhetoric where it refers to the final summing up when the speaker marshals his arguments, bringing them together in a definitive conclusion. In Jesus, we see God's final word on the original transgression that brought death and cascaded into violence and evil. Jesus is therefore God's 'summary statement'—

His Logos, His final rebuttal to the evil unleashed in the Garden of Eden.[88]

The focus of Irenaeus and subsequent commentators on redemption as a reversal of Adam's sin[89] obscures all the aspects of history Jesus mended during His life. To limit recapitulation to the crucifixion and resurrection misses the breathtaking splendour of the inversions and turnarounds Jesus accomplished during His ministry life. He didn't start the work of recapitulation at the Cross and He didn't finish it there either. Jesus was continually bringing healing to history. He was constantly remastering the plot of the events in the biblical chronicle, stitching up the wounds of the past and mending the ruptures in relationships across society that had existed for millennia. In doing so, He gives us the opportunity to choose a narrative of blessing, instead of brokenness.

Now, just as an aside, I don't want to be misunderstood. The following discussion is heavily reliant on several different theories of the atonement, including recapitulation, ransom, Christus Victor, satisfaction and substitution, all used in combination.[90] However, my primary focus is on the first three. Moreover, and most importantly, I am not restricting these concepts to the events surrounding the crucifixion and resurrection.

Now the first offensive of Jesus against Anat as described in the gospels occurs at the wedding feast of Cana. There, when the wine ran out, His mother informed Him of the situation, clearly hinting He should take action to protect the bridal party from shame and dishonour. However He responds to her that His hour has not yet come—it's not yet the appointed time for an epiphany, an unveiling of His identity and His glory.

But Mary simply goes to the servants and says:

> *'Do whatever He tells you.'*
>
> John 2:5 NIV

As mentioned previously, the only other time these words have ever been used in Scripture is in the story of Joseph. At the start of the seven-year famine the Egyptian people approach Pharaoh for food and he tells them to go to Joseph and:

> *'...do whatever he tells you.'*
>
> Genesis 41:55 NLT

John has a special technique for disabusing us of the thought this quote might be a coincidence. He uses a device of Hebrew poetry called 'chiasmus'—and he's created his gospel in this way with mirror reflections front and back. His words aren't symmetrical, but his concepts are. In the parallel position at the end of the gospel, there is another quote from the story of Joseph. Just as a mysterious stranger questions Joseph at Shechem as he's wandering around in search of his brothers, Jesus asks Mary Magdalene:

> *'Who*[91] *are you looking for?'*
> John 20:15 NLT; Genesis 37:15 NIV

With this in mind, how do the events of the wedding feast at Cana relate to Joseph and Anat? Remember: Joseph dispossessed the Egyptians and Anat is a spirit of both dispossession and appointed time. Also consider: the nature of the 'sign' Jesus provided at Cana is not primarily about a chemical transformation of water to wine, it's about time. Wine is mostly water that, over a period of months in a vine, combines with light and minerals to form grapes. Fermented grape juice becomes wine.

Jesus, the True Vine, the Light of the World and the Rock, turns months into minutes as water is transformed. Now from the clues John provides about the date, it is possible to ascertain that the wedding feast was held during the festival of Sukkot: that is, Tabernacles or Booths, usually in September or October.[92] Back more than a millennium previously this corresponded to Ra'shu Yeni,[93] the Canaanite New Wine Festival—when farmers were up to their knees in purple juice, commemorating the triumph of Anat wading up to her knees in the blood of her enemies.[94]

Look at what Jesus does: His sign is not just about timing, it's about new wine. He makes fine, mature wine, as attested by the tablemaster who expressed his surprise that the bridegroom had left the best wine until last. Paradoxically, however, it's also new wine—a word that, in Hebrew, is derived from a root meaning *dispossession* or *inheritance*. By producing new wine, Jesus promised to restore the inheritance of those who have been dispossessed. Yet, as He said, His hour had not yet come. So it was not the appointed time. He therefore summoned the appointed time to Himself, demonstrating His lordship over the very thing Anat claimed was hers to distribute.

His challenge to Anat was threefold:

- at the time of year when she was allegedly most powerful, He took the festival commemorating her acts of bloodshed and violence and ensured it was one of joy
- He took the name of the festival, Ra'shu Yeni, *First Wine*, and used it to point to Himself as the restorer of inheritance, thereby reversing Anat's agenda of dispossession and disappointment
- He called the appointed time to do His bidding, demonstrating that Anat had no claim over the sovereignty of time

A fourth aspect was His 'covering' of the bridegroom—there would have already been embarrassment and shame when the groom realised the wine was gone. Jesus provided a path for shame to be processed—as He would do later for the woman caught in adultery.

Three years later, the feast of Tabernacles has rolled around once more. Simon had just been dubbed

'Peter' by Jesus and had been taken, along with James and John, up a high mountain. But not just any high mountain—this was Mount Hermon, the place named for the curses thrown by the Watcher angels at each other to bind themselves into an agreement to seek beautiful human women as mates.

In my personal view, this was also the abode of the Canaanite divinities—the cosmic mountain where their palaces and temples, shrines and sanctuaries were situated. Now this identification is rarely that of professional scholarship who say that the mountain of the Canaanite assembly was Jebel Aqra, on the Syrian-Turkish border. Jebel Aqra, it is alleged, is Mount Zaphon where the palace of the storm-god Baal-Hadad was located.

Now the title 'Anat of Zaphon' is encoded in the name Pharaoh gave to Joseph and so identifying Zaphon as Mount Hermon has significant implications. I'm choosing to do so simply because of the actions of Jesus. However, I also want to point out that sacred mountains can walk. Well, not really, I exaggerate. But when people migrate from one place to another, the myths and stories attached to one mountain are transferred across to the nearest suitable peak in the new locality. So I believe that, as the Canaanites moved northwards on being displaced by the Israelites, so too did their sacred mountain that marked 'north'.

Zaphon not only means *north*, but also comes from a root for *covered, hidden* and for a *watch-tower, a look-out post*. This just as readily describes the snow-covered heights of Mount Hermon and its connection with the Watchers, as it does the peak of Jebel Aqra which is over 500 metres lower.

Now, because of the actions of Jesus after descending the mountain that I'll soon explain, it's clear He considered He'd climbed Zaphon. Here's why I think so:

Point one: there's no way Jesus could walk from Caesarea Philippi to Jebel Aqra in the six-day span[95] described in the gospels—it's over 250 kilometres in a straight line almost due north with some incredibly rough terrain to negotiate in between. By road today, it is almost twice as far. However He could have easily ascended Mount Hermon, since Caesarea Philippi lies in its foothills.

Point two: Zaphon is, according to Isaiah 14:13, the 'mount of assembly'. Now it's unclear which particular assembly this refers to.[96] Hermon is the 'mount of assembly of El'. That's not El, as in God as in Yahweh, but rather it's Bull El as in the chief of the Canaanite divinities. Jebel Aqra, on the other hand is the 'mount of assembly of Baal', that is, Hadad the storm-god who is the king amongst his seventy brothers and various sisters, but nonetheless who is still subject to Bull El.

Point three: these seventy brothers, sons of the goddess Asherah, were called 'the young lions'.

Point four: in order to fulfil the strange prophecy of Psalm 82 that God will stand up in the assembly of the gods—in fact, in their war council—Jesus had to declare Himself as God, or else be declared as God by the Father, at the 'mount of assembly'. Now we know that this happened at the Transfiguration because the Father announced: *'This is My beloved Son. Listen to Him.'* This proclamation was as much for the gathering of spirits as it was for the disciples. It is a complete counter to Anat's claim to be the judge of the gods in the sense that she is the kingmaker—the one most dominant in deciding who will be the ruler amongst the brothers. Yet in her very own sphere of influence, Yahweh the Father declares her choice of sovereign to be null and void.

Point five: Psalm 82 also prophesies that the judgment of God on the spiritual rulers of the nations (that is, the principalities, or 'young lions') will begin at that particular council when God shows up to pronounce a verdict on their reign. That decision, quite naturally, is that their time is up. They've failed to be righteous and have presided over injustice and abuse. Jesus begins to enact the verdict after He comes down the mountain. Shortly, not immediately but very soon, He dispatches seventy disciples out to preach the good news in the small villages of Galilee and Samaria. This is a highly symbolic action: *small villages* in Hebrew is exactly the same word as *young lions*. Nowhere else are seventy disciples sent out, so His action is indicative of the overthrow of the power of the principalities. This is not just recapitulation directed at the fall of the angelic shepherds—who are, by the way, distinct from the Watchers—but an exemplar of Christ as the victor against the great powers. He Himself testifies to this when He said He saw the satan fall as lightning from heaven.

Point six: Zion cannot be the 'mount of assembly' in this case because the Transfiguration does not happen in Jerusalem. It happens on a mountaintop less than six days' journey from Caesarea Philippi. It could therefore be Mount Tabor in Galilee, as is often suggested, but if that is the case, the sending out of the seventy disciples to the small villages has no symbolic overtones. It has no connotation of the overthrow of the seventy young lions, the principalities who rule the nations, that an ascent of Mount Hermon does.

Point seven: Elijah and Moses appeared together with Jesus during the Transfiguration. This is simply the most wondrous moment of it all, as far as I am concerned. Here, in the middle of a moment of stunning majestic glory, of mind-warping fall-down shock, of the delivery of a declaration of war, there's a scene of recapitulation that is weighty with overwhelming compassion, measureless mercy and splendiferous forgiveness. Moses had died some fifteen centuries previously and had never made it to the Promised Land. After he'd struck the rock—symbolising his refusal of covenant with God—the Lord had barred him from entering the land. In effect, Moses chose not to *draw water* as God told him to by speaking to the rock, an action related to his own name, thereby showing he was still unwilling to give up his Egyptian heritage. God, however, was insisting Moses cross the Jordan and enter the land as a Hebrew, not an Egyptian. As soon as God said no, Moses tried to bargain:

> *'Let me go over and see the good land beyond the Jordan—that fine hill country and Lebanon.'*
>
> Deuteronomy 3:25 NIV

What he'd asked for was permission to *go around*, not across the Jordan River: to travel up to the hill country of Lebanon, circle the headwaters of the Jordan and enter the country that way. But God said:

> *'That is enough... Do not speak to Me anymore about this matter.'*
>
> Deuteronomy 3:26 NIV

And yet, and yet, and yet—Jesus is truly Yes and Amen, for Moses has been given what he requested. He is in the fine hill country of Lebanon. And he's there with Jesus.

If that's not wonderful enough, let's consider the situation of Elijah, the prophet who feared Anat of Zaphon so greatly that he abandoned his calling and did not carry out the tasks God had assigned to him. But he appears with Jesus, on Zaphon, on the mount of assembly, in the middle of a war council of the young lions he'd been so terrified of. With Jesus, everything changes. Elijah had been more fearful of Anat than he'd been of Yahweh, but now that dread is swept away in the company of Jesus.

And Jesus was not just taking on the principalities—those angels who had been given rulership of the nations and who subsequently fell into corruption. He also began the work of overturning the transgression of the Watchers—those greater powers whose sin had resulted in the giants who had drowned in the flood and whose hybrid angelic-human spirits became the demons.

Jesus finished the original assignment given to Elijah—the overthrow of the government in the northern kingdom—Samaria, including Galilee. Had Elijah followed through on his prophetic task after the triumph at Mount Carmel then, instead of running from Jezebel, he would have instructed Obadiah to usher the hundred prophets out of the caves where they were hidden. They would have soon discovered they were just a small fraction of the 7000 who had never bowed to Baal. Do the calculation: there could have been 100 companies of 70 people, all loyal to Yahweh, travelling throughout the land and calling people back to God. Look at what Jesus did with just one company. Imagine the blessing of a hundred of them.

In completing that unfinished work of Elijah, Jesus was directly opposing the power that had taken the prophet down in the first place. There were many spirits ranged against Elijah but the tip of the spear in their ranks was Anat of Zaphon.

As He was speaking, the teachers of religious law and the Pharisees brought a woman who had been caught in the act of adultery. They put her in front of the crowd.

'Teacher,' they said to Jesus, 'this woman was caught in the act of adultery. The law of Moses says to stone her. What do You say?'

They were trying to trap him into saying something they could use against him, but Jesus stooped down and wrote in the dust with His finger. They kept demanding an answer, so He stood up again and said, 'All right, but let the one who has never sinned throw the first stone!' Then He stooped down again and wrote in the dust.

When the accusers heard this, they slipped away one by one, beginning with the oldest, until only Jesus was left in the middle of the crowd with the woman. Then Jesus stood up again and said to the woman, 'Where are your accusers? Didn't even one of them condemn you?'

'No, Lord,' she said.

And Jesus said, 'Neither do I. Go and sin no more.'
John 8:3–11 NLT

The shame must have been overwhelming, intolerable, excruciating. And when, for us in our own situations, we've been similarly exposed for wrongdoing—and we have no way to process a humiliation that is beyond endurance—we seek desperately and instinctively for a covering. Just as Adam and Eve did when they first knew shame. Normally it will be prideful self-righteousness, leading to narcissism; or it will be prideful shamelessness, leading to addiction.

Instead of turning to Jesus and covering ourselves in His righteousness through repentance, we turn to Lilith and accept her offering with its concealed in-built abuse. As noted previously, Jesus does not speak of forgiveness in this scene. It's too late for it when shame has taken hold and the shattered soul is mired in the belief it is defective and irreparably soiled, worthless, born faulty, unfixable. He is instead clear that He does not condemn—implying a need for repentance when He tells her not to sin again.

He differentiates between shame and guilt: between *being* wrong and *doing* wrong. And He offers a pathway out of shame, out of addiction, out of narcissism. When I was preparing this book, I consulted many professionals. It had dawned on me that, if it were possible to turn shame into guilt, then there was an easy way forward. Guilt, after all, is dealt with through Spirit-empowered repentance. However all the literature seemed to suggest turning shame to guilt was impossible. All the experts I spoke to agreed. So I sighed and finally said to God that I guessed there are just some things we have to accept as unachievable. So, unpleasant as it was, I would simply get on with acknowledging that as a fact of life.

God allowed this disheartening thought to saturate my mind for two days before He said, 'Jesus died to make this possible.'

I immediately threw off my cloak of gloomy acceptance and began to pray He'd show me how it could be done. For three solid months I prayed, getting no answer. And then, one day, I was in prayer ministry with a new person and I realised unresolved shame was exactly her problem. *I need the answer now*, I thought at God. *Right now*.

And to buy myself a bit of time because the answer still wasn't coming, I explained to the woman all about guilt and shame and the difference between them. She absolutely agreed that her problem was that she believed she'd been a mistake from birth, she was damaged goods, a failed creation. Nothing she did was right. Everything was wrong because she was stupid. Her shame was intense and she could at last see it was the root cause of her past addictions and narcissistic tendencies.

Holy Spirit, we're out of time, I was thinking to myself. *I need the answer now. How do you turn shame into guilt?*

'Just ask Me,' He whispered.

Just ask Him?

My thoughts were upended in disbelief. *It couldn't possibly be that easy, could it?* I took a deep breath. Nothing ventured, nothing gained. It was simple enough that, if it didn't work, nothing was lost.

So I looked at the woman and said, 'I'm going to pray and, with your agreement, we're going to ask Jesus to turn shame into guilt. And when we've done that, I want you to repeat after me: I am not stupid, I did something stupid. I am not a mistake, I made a mistake. I am not rotten, I sometimes do bad things.'

According to Jonathan Sacks, the Jewish faith is the supreme example of a guilt-and-repentance culture, as opposed to the shame-and-honour culture of the ancient Greeks.[97] Other shame-and-honour cultures include Japanese, Chinese and other Asian cultures as well as Palestinian. In these societies, evil is seen as attached to the person. In a guilt-and-righteousness culture, evil is seen as attached to sinful action. A guilt culture hates the sin, not the sinner. Repentance is always possible, because the person has a sacred self that remains intact.[98]

Still, in today's world, Sacks points out, 'Emotions like guilt, shame, contrition and remorse have been deleted from our vocabulary, for are we not all entitled to self-esteem?'[99]

Yet these emotions are the very core of the scene involving the woman caught in adultery. It's my belief she was Mary of Bethany, the sister of Jesus' friend Lazarus. If the shame of being dragged in front of strangers was unbearable, how much more so would it have been in front of your brother's friend—the rabbi you'd so admired that you wanted nothing better than to sit at His feet and listen to His teaching?

Now the reason I think they are the same person is because Mary of Bethany is the one who cracks open the alabaster jar of precious oil to anoint Jesus with spikenard and myrrh. Her actions of washing His travel-stained feet with her tears and wiping them with her hair tells us:

- she's either completely shameless—thus this is an action that dishonours Jesus—*or*
- she's learned how to process shame and is so far beyond it that she doesn't care if she's embarrassed in offering Jesus the honour that is His due
- she's so immeasurably grateful to Jesus that the words and thoughts of those who despise her are not relevant and their scathing criticisms cannot affect her.

The woman caught in adultery fits these criteria. Now Mary could have done this in private and avoided all the contention and derision. That's from a human point-of-view. But from God's perspective, it was absolutely necessary she do it in public.

With this action, she becomes the antitype to Anat in her role as kingmaker of the gods.[100] The anointing takes place at Bethany—sometimes thought to be Jeremiah's hometown of Anathoth, named for Anat.[101] It occurs on the evening before—that is, the same day in Jewish reckoning—Jesus triumphantly enters Jerusalem on a donkey. He is the Son of David, recapitulating the ride of Solomon, son of David, as the people rejoiced and shouted as he made his way through the streets to his coronation.

Now two important elements were needed for the proclamation of a king in ancient Israel: costly anointing oil as well as living water, that is, water that flows and is not stagnant. Solomon was anointed king by Zadok the priest and Nathan the prophet. Jesus, on other hand, was anointed king by Mary of Bethany who used the most precious of oils and the flowing water of her tears in the ceremony.

He defended her against her critics, saying:

> *Truly I tell you, wherever the gospel is preached throughout the world, what she has done will also be told, in memory of her.*
>
> Mark 14:9 NIV

At this moment, I believe, Jesus gave her a new identity: the Magdalene. Until He says these words, she's simply Mary, the sister of Lazarus and Martha, or Mary of Bethany. Afterwards, she's Mary *the* Magdalene—not Mary of Magdala, but rather Mary the Magdalene. That's the way Scripture records her:

Mary the Magdalene, Mary the memorial, Mary the watchtower, Mary the preserver of memory.

Her story—the story of Mary the kingmaker—is a memorial in its own right to the coronation of Jesus. It's a verbal monument created so that future generations will not forget a special moment in history. Memorials are about *memory*. The name Mary has multiple meanings but one of them is perched out on a branch of the same tree of words to which *memory* and *memorial* belong. Also part of this tree is 'Samaria', which means *watchtower*.[102]

In fact, both Samaritan and Magdalene mean *of the watchtower*. See how cleverly Jesus played with these words. He appointed Mary as the Deborah of her age—Anat's opponent. But, to protect her, He kept it under wraps.

Anat of Zaphon means, among other things, *eye*—or *fountain*—*of the watchtower*. The dual meaning *eye* and *fountain* is sometimes thought to refer to *tears*.

Mary the Magdalene means, among other things, *salty water* *of the watchtower*.

Tears of *the watchtower* vs *salty water* of *the watchtower:* not much to choose between the two. Still, it's sufficiently concealed that Mary's role as the Deborah of the first century is not immediately apparent. Had that been realised by the spiritual powers opposing Jesus, she would have been an instant target. Like Deborah, she is called to be a partner in drawing out the enemy onto the battleground of God's choosing, so He can accomplish the victory. Her role is not simply to be a witness and a living repository of memory, but to participate at a crucial moment in the finale.

When Jesus spoke over her at the dinner, naming her action as a perpetual memorial wherever the gospel is preached, He gifted her with a new identity. It's a parallel to God speaking over us at conception, whispering a name to us and breathing into us identity and destiny.

In the normal birth process, conception must be followed by implantation within six days. So it was for the Magdalene that six days later[103] all the events of the Passover occurred. This is the time period when her new identity must be implanted or it will be naturally lost. If she is everything Anat of Zaphon is not, then she has to take part in a recapitulation that reworks Anat's story, going over it so that the rips are mended and the ruptures are healed.

Her role on the day of the crucifixion and especially the resurrection is multi-faceted—first, she is the representative of humanity who goes looking for God in a garden, in contrast to the events of Eden where God comes looking for humanity. Second, her language is reminiscent of the bridal scene in the Song of Songs and, third, it reflects the words of Anat as she searches for her brother Hadad so she can bring him back from the dead.

The words of Jesus to Mary in the garden outside the tomb are superficially simple and natural: *'Who are you looking for?'* Yet they go back to the story of Joseph as he is searching for his brothers—to a time before the first recorded Scriptural instance of dispossession of property and land rights occurred, to the time before Joseph himself received a new name and identity, to the time before Anat so thoroughly achieved her purpose of transferring our inheritance to her own account.

And we can be absolutely sure Jesus had Anat in His sights as He conversed with Mary. *'Woman,'* He asked, *'why are you crying?'* [104] Undoubtedly He spoke in Aramaic. And the word for *woman* in Aramaic is 'anath'.

Just, as it so happens, another way of spelling Anat.

It's the work of God to turn our *dis*appointments into His appointments. It's the work of God to tackle shame on our behalf, as He did for Adam and Eve.

In *The Voyage of the 'Dawn Treader'*, Eustace has to submit to undressing by the great lion so his many layers of dragonskin can be permanently removed. It's the same with us and shame: there are layers upon unending layers to remove—the different cloaks we wear, the masks, and all the screens and projections of narcissistic, self-righteous covering.

Just as Joseph dispossessed the Egyptians and gave them no way to regain their inheritance, so Anat blocks the processing of shame so there is no way to regain a true sense of self. The blockage is so high and wide and long, we can't overcome it. Sometimes, even though it's so extensive, our denial is so extreme we aren't even aware the shame exists. Until God exposes it.

He has made a way forward for us, if only we have the courage to accept it. We can choose to repress it once again when God brings shame to the light, or we can face the fear and pain of being undragoned.

Just ask Me.

That's what God said in response to my prayer about a process for turning shame into guilt, so that the guilt can then be dealt with through repentance and the covering of the Cross. 'You lucked out,' was the attitude of most of the people I knew when I told them what had happened. They didn't believe it would work except in very rare cases. But slowly their skepticism changed as God all but cornered them into trying it. It's certainly not always an easy process, because shame is so resistant to exposure—but it's worth pushing on through the pain.[105] When the moment of breakthrough comes, so many people wondered why they waited so long to ask Him in the first place.

The gospels of Matthew and Mark both mention that Mary the Magdalene was present at the crucifixion.

Matthew adds in the apparently minor detail she sat with another Mary. But it's not minor—it's integral to her identification as the new Deborah. She has to sit at a 'tree of weeping' like that where Deborah the nurse was buried and where Deborah the judge spoke her prophecies.

The Romans were to turn the entire iconography of the warrior woman judge on its head several decades later. They issued coins after the conquering of Jerusalem, stamped with the words 'Iudea capta', *Judea captive*, and with the image of a woman who represented the defeated nation, sitting and mourning under a palm tree alongside the armour of the conquered Jews.[106]

John's gospel not only confirms the Magdalene's presence at the Cross but is the only account to include details of her conversation with Peter and himself, as well as Jesus, after the resurrection. This is critical information. Without it, we would not know that Jesus had given her Deborah's mantle—a legacy that went all the way back to Joseph and that needed serious restoration because of the taint of dispossession clinging to it.

Twice the Magdalene mentions that Jesus has been taken away—*lifted, raised* is the word she uses—and she doesn't know where He has been put: *appointed, set in place, established*. These are truly ambiguous words. John makes it clear that he and Simon Peter didn't really believe Jesus would rise from the dead, but these words give the impression the Magdalene may well have had a different view.

Ironically, when the Magdalene puts the question concerning the whereabouts of Jesus to Jesus Himself she fails the first test of a guardian appointed to a watchtower. A watchman has to be able to recognise friend from foe. Yet Jesus had to reveal Himself to her.

However the repetition of her question within the gospel narrative is a clue as to how significant it is. In this despoiling of Canaanite religious liturgy, it parallels the repeated question of Anat as she searches for the body of Baal-Hadad: *'Where is the prince?' 'Where is the lord?'*

In the rites of Hadad, this question was used as a ritual call. The worshippers would gather outside a cave at the end of winter, repeating this cry to encourage Baal to emerge from his long sojourn in the underworld. But the words originally were spoken by Anat of Zaphon in the epic story of her search for Baal after he'd been killed by Mot, *Death*.

Anat's claim to be the revivifier of the dead is overturned by Jesus in His recapitulation of the story: the Magdalene searches for Him at the resurrection, asking essentially the same question as Anat, but she has no part whatsoever in His return to life. And even though she had a monumental role in His appointment as an earthly king, she has none at all in His induction as the priest-king of heaven. In fact, she's told not to touch Jesus because He has not yet presented Himself to the Father. His words, *'Do not touch Me for not yet have I ascended to the Father,'*[107] evoke the repeated warning of the high priest on the Day of Atonement as he was about to enter the Holy of Holies and sprinkle blood on the mercy seat of the Ark of the Covenant: 'Do not touch Me with anything of this world for I have not yet been with the Father.'[108] Jesus was about to present His own blood—that of the perfect once-for-all sacrifice—in heaven and, until He has been accepted as the Eternal High Priest, He needs to maintain ritual cleanness.[109] No one can touch Him.

'Where is the lord?' is not only the essence of the Magdalene's question concerning the whereabouts of Jesus and it's not only a commemoration of words of Anat by the liturgy of Baal-Hadad, it's also the basis of the name Jezebel.

Here Jesus deals with the healing of a bloodline. Jezebel is the mother of Athaliah—named in an apparent compromise for both Anat and Yahweh—who marries the king of Judah. Athaliah is the queen mother who seizes the opportunity to take the throne after the death of her son Ahaziah. She's therefore in the ancestral tree of Jesus, and so too is Jezebel. His mending of that aspect of history is encompassed within His complete takedown of the spiritual powers behind Jezebel and Athaliah—Anat and her brother Baal-Hadad as well as their mother Asherah. Jesus demonstrates His right to one of

Asherah's most significant titles, 'She Who Walks On Water', when He simply steps out onto the surface of the Sea of Galilee to meet up with His disciples who are out on the lake in a boat.[110]

The dialogue between Jesus and Mary is so simple that it belies the rich complexity and the historical weight it carries. The bell-like echoes of Eden, the Song of Songs, the Marriage of the Lamb, the stories of Joseph and Jezebel, Athaliah and Deborah all ring in jubilation at the reversals of tragedy and the fulfilment of prophecy. Yet the war of Jesus against the powers didn't finish at the Cross: it's still going on here as He obliterates every claim of the Canaanite pantheon, taking back for Himself and for His Father the rewards of conquest including usurped titles and names, liturgical formulations, symbols and rituals. He also lays hold of a storyline involving a return from death after a stay in the underworld. It's total despoilation, nothing less.

Baal-Hadad the Cloud-rider, Anat and her sister Myrrh, Mot the death-lord, Bull El, Asherah and all the others who so terrified Elijah and the other prophets are put in their place—their appointed place. And we need to keep asking Jesus to return them there.

The Jews then responded to Him, 'What sign can You show us to prove Your authority to do all this?'

> *Jesus answered them, 'Destroy this Temple, and I will raise it again in three days.'*
>
> *They replied, 'It has taken forty-six years to build this Temple, and You are going to raise it in three days?' But the Temple He had spoken of was His body.*
>
> John 2:18–21 NIV

The Jewish leaders challenged Jesus when He drove the money-changers out of the Temple to produce His authority. His answer that, in three days, He would rebuild the destroyed Temple basically amounted to: 'Wait a week and My credentials will be completely obvious.' In referring to the Temple of His body, He announced that He was the fulfilment of all the Temple represented.[111] In conquering Anat so decisively, He showed she had no place in Him and He had no place in her.

It's incredibly important for this to sink into every tiny recess, crack and crevice of our hearts. The truth is: we dwell in Christ and He does in us. However, there are sly corners of our being that have listened to Anat's counterfeit claim that she is in us and we are in her. It's not enough to sever our complicity with Anat in whatever guise she appears—Lilith, Neith, Athena, Hebat, Hannahannah, Inanna, Ishtar, Minerva—unless we address the double bond.

Jesus was the true blueprint of the Temple. In addition to being its fulfilment, He was also its tested, precious Cornerstone as well as its Foundation, as Isaiah had prophesied.[112]

In the inner court were the Menorah with its seven branches of light, the table with the Bread of the Presence on it, and the altar of incense where prayers were offered. The throne guardian Leviathan corresponds to these items—but, when Jesus took His rightful place, He showed how these items represented Him. He is the Light of the World,[113] the Bread of Life[114] and the perfect Mediator who presents our prayers to the Father.[115] He is the Gate of the Sheep[116] and the Living Water[117]—the Temple gates and bronze washing laver correspond to these aspects of His identity. He is the Passover and also the Lamb of God,[118] slain before the foundation of the world. His is the blood that ends forever the need for further sacrifice and He is also the High Priest[119] who offers this blood of the new covenant in atonement.

Totally comprehensive. No stone left unturned.

Jesus made everything available to us: we can live in Him and He is us. And He'll give us His kiss to armour us and He'll be our covenant defender and no weapon formed against us will prevail.

And if you think Anat is going to take this lying down, think again. She's eyed off what Jesus did to reverse the wounds of history through His stunning work of recapitulation and decided, as she did with her brother Hadad, that whatever Jesus can do she can do better. He might have defeated her, she might be down for the count but she's not out and not dead, and she fights dirty. She's intent on reversing the reversals, overturning the recapitulations and upending the healings. She's made it her mission to ensure that, whatever you ask for in prayer, you get the exact opposite.

When I first heard of believers getting inversions of what they asked for in prayer, I was completely baffled. It seemed impossible. Jesus, after all, said:

> *'Would any of you who are fathers give your son a snake when he asks for fish? Or would you give him a scorpion when he asks for an egg? As bad as you are, you know how to give good things to your children. How much more, then, will the Father in heaven give the Holy Spirit to those who ask Him!'*
>
> Luke 11:11–13 GNT

In the past, I'd prayed for people who reacted to this verse with the thought that it might be true for others, but not for them. Because of experiences with their earthly fathers, they couldn't believe God would bless them. It wasn't that they thought they'd get the scorpion, but rather that the egg would be rotten. Still, once they'd repented of believing this lie, His favour was overflowing and miraculous.

Receiving a reversal as a response to prayer is different from 'no' or 'not yet'. It's the very antithesis of grace.

On the surface it might seem a bit like retaliation—like Leviathan in operation, or since it involves prayer, like the work of Resheph—one of Leviathan's 'faces' or 'heads'. But the legal rights in these instances derive from dishonour. Moreover, at least in the case of Resheph, there'll be no mistake about the source of the dishonour because it will be so swift in coming. The time lag between cause and effect, between the instance of dishonour in prayer and the repercussions, will be almost non-existent.

These reversals just didn't make sense. How could any spirit interfere with God's grace at this level?

It was only when I heard of the practice of Egyptian spiritualism,[120] with its attempts to deliver upside-down, inside-out, back-to-front results through the power of the ancient gods that it began to make sense.

Anat may be Canaanite in origin but, in the Bible, the first two episodes that show the depth of her influence happen in Egypt. It isn't simply that the people of Egypt were dispossessed by Joseph when they came to petition him for food, it's that he used the stockpiles of grain *that they themselves had provided in earlier years* as the leverage tool to compel them to agree.

Here we see Anat as the spirit of dispossession working in strong alliance with Belial. One of the hallmarks of Belial, the spirit of abuse, is: *you will resource the war against yourself.*

Anat, in her vampire aspect as Lilith, sucks life in order to reinforce abuse by ensuring our own spiritual power is used against us.

Prayer

The following two prayers may be unbelievably hard to say. Even with the backing of Jesus, we may find it almost impossible to shunt the shame of being ashamed enough to the side to be able to speak these words. The inability to sideline the shame of being ashamed comes directly from pride, not from any sense of unworthiness or worthlessness. We often try to tackle shame, before tackling the pride standing in the way of being able to acknowledge the shame.

Please be specific in addressing wrongdoing. As Joe Medina has said, 'We must name our sin in order to tame our sin.'[121]

Prayer for the Shame of *DOING* Wrong

Heavenly Father, I clothe myself each day in the thought, 'I am right.' And sometimes I rephrase it, 'I am not wrong.'

The hardest thing on earth to admit is: 'I *am* not wrong but I *did* wrong,' and then to ask You to help me repent of what I did. Because it's true I *am* not wrong, I *am* not defective, I *am* not worthless, I *am* not unrepairable—but I don't really believe that. To admit that I did *do* wrong feels like saying I *am* wrong. And although it isn't, my soul isn't convinced. It feels like a betrayal of self to say, 'I *am* not wrong but I am guilty of *doing* wrong. I am not guilty of *being* wrong, I am guilty of *doing* wrong.'

I thank Jesus of Nazareth for providing a way, through His cross, of removing the guilt of *doing* wrong, even though I find it impossible to move into that space. I acknowledge that I have not chosen His way but have let shame cover me with the self-righteous thought, 'I am right.'

I have not reached for the cover of the righteousness of Jesus through confessing: 'I am not wrong but I did wrong.' I acknowledge that I have blamed others to bolster my self-righteousness.

I ask You, Jesus, to turn my shame into guilt.

I ask You to change the shame of *being* wrong, defective, worthless, unrepairable into the guilt of *doing* wrong and missing the mark.

I ask You to grant me the ability to say aloud, 'I did wrong but that does not mean to say I am made wrong.' I also ask Him to place a sign in my mind as a permanent fixture: *my behaviour is not me.*

I accept Jesus' gift of redemption through the grace of guilt and repentance. I therefore say, naming specific moments: 'I am guilty of doing ...., but I repent of my sinful behaviour. I repent of the pride that kept me from seeking the help of Jesus before this. I ask Him, through His blood that mediates for me in heaven, to empower these words of repentance to achieve the change He has won for me. I ask Him to strengthen my will so I will not do this again. I ask Him to remove my covering of shame and self-righteousness, scrub me clean of addictions, wash me in the waters of repentance, refreshment and renewal through the work of the Holy Spirit, anoint me with the fragrant oil that appoints me to the position of authority He wants me to exercise, clothe me in His own freshly-laundered, sweet-smelling garments of righteousness, place on my shoulder the keys He wants me to use in opening the right doors, and put around my neck the seal of the office He wants me to assume.

I thank You, Jesus, and I praise You for enabling me to overcome the enemy's plans for me by releasing me from my cage of shame.

In Jesus' name. Amen.

Prayer for the Shame of *BEING* Wrong

This is how I feel and how I can't unfeel: I *am* wrong.

I am not right.

I am not right, so I should have no rights.

I am not right because someone who should have loved me blamed me for not being what they wanted.

I am not right because my existence, as I am in the way I am, was never wanted.

I am not right unless I cease to be, but that is not right either. So I'm stuck in my permanent unchangeable not-rightness and I cover my shame for the not-rightness by striving to make up for my inadequacy. But it's impossible for someone who is not right in the very essence of their being to do right, so my attempts never work and my shame deepens. All the cycle does is produce more shame.

When the Lord says to me, 'You are My chosen, My treasure, My beloved,' I look around to see who's standing behind me because I know He can't mean me.

I am always repenting, always forgiving, always confessing, always renouncing because I can never clear myself of the wrongness and shame within. Yet there's one thing I can't seem to repent of: the belief that God made everything good—*except me*. I'm the exception and maybe there's just a touch of secret pride in being unique like that. I can forgive those who blamed me for being not what they wanted but I can't forgive myself for being wrong. I try to do that, but it doesn't work. I try to tell myself that it doesn't work because it's futile to forgive myself for my wrongness, when God actually tells me I don't have any wrongness of being. But His words just don't stick. I can forgive myself for doing wrong but not for being wrong. The one thing I can't remove is the shame I've taken on. I'm too ashamed to let Jesus have my shame and cover me with His righteousness. What if He lets people see who I really am in that process?

Lord Jesus of Nazareth, I'm scared to hand over my covering of shame because I'm terrified it will leave me even more naked and vulnerable and exposed. So, Lord, if I have to be dragged in front of You like the woman caught in adultery, I give permission for Your angels to pull me there. I ask You to help me process the shame I experience and accept Your truth about who I am and who I was made to be. I ask You to take the shame, even when I try to hold on to it.

In all my acts of repentance and forgiveness there are some critical things I've missed. These are the things I need to repent of *doing*, not of *being*. I name them before You and ask You to accept my confession through my mediator, Jesus of Nazareth:

I repent of accepting the dishonour projected on to me and of allowing it to be part of the foundation of my identity.

I repent of believing the lie that I shouldn't exist as I am and that, to be acceptable, I needed to conform to another person's impossible desires.

I repent of trying to appease another person's dissatisfaction with the way You made me instead of looking to You for my identity.

I repent of my agreement with the lie that I am not worthy, that I'm a mistake, that I'm defective, that I'm damaged goods. I might not be what another person wanted or 'ordered' but I am who You made me to be.

I repent of taking on the shame that was pressed onto me and into me, and of trying to be someone other than I am in order to cover that shame.

I repent of trying to be invisible so that my wrongness would not be noticed, and then feeling left out when no one acknowledged my presence or existence.

I repent of turning myself inside out in an impossible attempt to please someone who would not accept Your will.

I repent of submitting to their arrogance and to their prideful belief that they knew what was best, instead of submitting to You.

I forgive them for that arrogance and I forgive myself for bowing before it.

I forgive those who were disappointed in me for not meeting their needs.

I forgive those who overlooked me, ignored me, dishonoured me, humiliated me, ridiculed me and exalted themselves by shaming me.

I ask You, Heavenly Father, to forgive all my efforts to reinvent myself to please someone other than You. I ask Jesus to empower my words of repentance and to give life to my words of forgiveness, to hide me under the shadow of the wing of His prayer shawl as He dissolves my shame and to clothe me there in the soft glow of His righteousness. I know His righteousness is dazzling but I'd just like to tiptoe out in a soft glow, please, until I'm sure it's quite safe.

I speak to my own heart now and to my belly and I say to them: 'It's a new day. Believe Jesus when He says I am perfect in His sight. Get over yourself. Who is the King of the Universe, and Lord of me—is it Jesus, or the one who blamed me for not fulfilling their needs? Who should judge my rightness or wrongness—Jesus, or the one who would not accept God's will?'

I choose the love of Jesus. I choose the vindication of Jesus. I choose the verdict of Jesus. I choose the rightness and righteousness of Jesus. I choose Jesus.

Kiss me with Your armour of light and let me know who I really am. I accept, from now on, that I sometimes *do* wrong but I no longer accept that I *am* wrong.

> In the name of Jesus of Nazareth
> and through the power of His atoning blood.
> Amen.

4

Armament for Battle

The fruit of the Spirit is love, joy, peace, patience, kindness, goodness, faithfulness, gentleness, self-control; against such things there is no law.

Galatians 5:22–23 ESV

PAUL WROTE TO THE GALATIANS—a Celtic people living in Asia Minor who were famed for providing mercenaries to various royal courts—giving them an understanding of how to inherit the kingdom of God. This was a warrior culture and Paul is talking weaponry.

We tend to miss that nuance. We overlook the fact that the Fruit of the Spirit is not merely a sevenfold set of character traits but an armament depot. If you were taught in Sunday School that the Fruit of the Spirit is ninefold, you might already be querying which ones I've ditched from the lineup. The answer is: none at all.

If you've read other books in this series, you will know that I believe the only reason Paul mentioned nine instead of seven was because there was no suitable single translation for the Hebrew word 'chesed'—so he used three Greek words for it. They are the ones we translate as *kindness, goodness* and *faithfulness*. It isn't a problem that was unique to Paul. When Myles Coverdale was translating the Bible, he encountered the same dilemma and rendered 'chesed' as *loving kindness*, a terminology later adopted by the translators of the King James Version who made a single word of the combination.

It may seem strange to begin with to think of the Fruit of the Spirit as munitions. But a moment's reflection will hopefully make it all clear. The most basic spiritual principle of the universe is: *you reap what you sow*. Paul, obviously still thinking about spiritual farming, mentions this soon after he describes the Fruit of the Spirit:

> *Do not be deceived: God is not mocked, for whatever one sows, that will he also reap.*
>
> Galatians 6:7 ESV

The sowing-and-reaping axiom works both positively and negatively, for blessing and for trouble. However we tend to notice the impact of the negative side more. In fact, it's so obvious that it's been expressed in various ways by numerous cultures, all with slightly different overtones: as karma, kismet, nemesis, cause and effect, law of consequences, something that comes back to bite us or the observation that 'what goes around comes around'. In the scientific age, this ancient understanding of the way the spiritual world operates has its counterpart in the action-reaction rule of physics.

This principle doesn't just apply to humanity even though, in some senses, it looks like a crude and simple application of the 'eye for an eye, tooth for a tooth' rule. God doesn't have one fundamental statute of justice for humanity and another for the angelic world. They too have to reap what they've sown.

Now way back in the Garden of Eden, fruit was weaponised against humanity. As a consequence, under the sowing-and-reaping principle, the reverse is true. Fruit was weaponised by the enemy, so Fruit is now weaponised against him—and his allies.

But the Fruit of the Spirit doesn't spring into being, fully formed. It begins as a seed, grows as we water it with the Word and as God gives the increase, and finally it becomes mature through trying and testing. These trials are necessary—how, for example, can a person be judged as honest unless they are tempted to be dishonest? How can a person be judged as pure, unless they've been tempted to immorality? Innocence is not the same as purity. Innocence can never be regained but purity can.

The trials are not only necessary, so are the failures that accompany them. It takes us a long time to reach the conclusion that we're never going to pass the trials without the help of Jesus. By that time, we've also realised that He always seems to stand back when the trial is in progress—we're asking God to save us but He seems to be silent. It's important to understand that God will not make a choice for us. That would violate free will. He won't tell us what to do. That would make the choice His, not ours, and the test would be worthless. If, however, we ask Him for guidance as to the most loving action in particular circumstances, or how to show kindness in a way that won't be misunderstood, then He'll help us. We've already made a choice at that point—we want to go with love but we're unsure what it should look like in our present situation and so we go to Him presenting that choice but acknowledging our inability to bring the choice to pass.

The fully tested and mature Fruit of the Spirit are peerless and practical weapons. As noted in previous books, however, it's important to identify which threshold spirit we're facing. Deploying *patience* against Python is simply playing into its hands. Lobbing *joy* at Azazel is counterproductive. Hurling *gentleness* at Leviathan will have a reasonable effect, but *peace* would be so much more efficient.

When it comes to tactical strategy, *love* works best against Python, *joy* against Ziz, *peace* against Leviathan and Resheph, *patience* against Rachab, *kindness*, *goodness* and *faithfulness* against Belial and Kronos, *self-control* against Azazel and *gentleness* against Lilith and Anat.

But these are not fleshly kinds of virtue. Unless we view them from God's perspective, not the world's, then we'll fall into the trap that He wants to empower us to avoid.

Now although the weaponisation of the fruit in the Garden resulted in the Fruit of the Spirit becoming armaments, this is not the end of the story. In response, Anat weaponised the Word of God. We can see this in the life of Jesus when He was tempted by the devil who quoted Psalm 91 in order to persuade Him to jump from the pinnacle of the Temple.

> *For He will command His angels concerning you to guard you in all your ways; they will lift you up in their hands, so that you will not strike your foot against a stone.*
>
> Psalm 91:11–12 NIV

This weaponisation of Scripture is a diabolical dare. Like most similar words directed at us, it implicitly calls our faith and courage into question. Deep humility is required to stand against such manipulation of God's Word—because we will quickly be accused of lacking trust in God. Our pride rushes to our defence, urging us to give way to the pressure, and to stop us from being shamed, as well as being seen as weak and cowardly.

Instead of leaving our reputations in God's hands, we allow ourselves to be manipulated by what others think of us.

Our powerlessness against an entity as ferocious as Anat is one factor in luring us into a truce with her. Another is our doubt that we can depend on Jesus to defend us against her. And a third is the even greater doubt that the most effective weapon against her is gentleness—that Fruit of the Spirit also called meekness. Or humility.

No, we think to ourselves, that can't possibly be right. Meekness equals weakness. Humility involves grovelling abasement. Gentleness is faint and feeble. These are the messages of our age.

So, we think, surely we have to strongarm Anat, show her the might of the Lord operating through our faith. How can we not have to fight, just as judges like Shamgar and Samson did? Though, naturally, we have to learn from their mistakes.

> *Shamgar son of Anath became judge. He also delivered Israel, striking down six hundred Philistines with a cattle prod.*
>
> Judges 3:31 CSB

Now, if *gentleness* is what overcomes this spirit—then Samson and Shamgar were not going the right way about overcoming her. They simply fell for the trap. Samson, in particular, might have been humiliated when he was outsmarted by the Philistines who guessed the riddle[123] he posed at his wedding, but instead of turning to God to overcome his sense of shame, he used God's Spirit to build himself up into battle rage. Later, his answer to shame was shamelessness, not humility. He went to Gaza to visit a prostitute, then pulled himself out of the hostile situation he found himself in by manipulating threshold covenant. Only when he learned humility was he able to connect with God again.

We've been taught by our culture to despise the one weapon that will enable us to stand effectively against Anat. We've been persuaded that the controlled strength of gentleness means niceness and softness, compliance and sweetness. Actually, it looks more like Deborah on the top of Mount Tabor with Barak and ten thousand farmers.[122]

Recall that Anat's name is related to words for *poor, humble* and *meek*. Her original office as one of the elohim was to demonstrate to humanity the virtues of humility and meekness. She's turned that around and, rather than strength under control, she exhibits uncontrolled and vicious might. Yet God has overturned her violence and expects us to use the very meekness she was supposed to display against her. In part, His purpose is that:

> *Now, through the church, the manifold wisdom of God should be made known to the rulers and authorities in the heavenly realms.*
>
> Ephesians 3:10 NIV

God's basic strategy with Anat and her allies—be they human or spirit—is for us to draw out the enemy. So He can fight on our behalf. It doesn't matter how belligerent a dozen farmers on the top of Mount Tabor are, they are simply not a sufficient threat to draw the enemy into position. Ten thousand, on the other hand, don't need to demonstrate any force of arms—they just need to show up.

Sisera's death is a prime example of the sowing-and-reaping principle. He is believed to have been a worshipper of Astarte—Anat's sister—in the era before Anat and Astarte were basically fused together into a religious unity. Astarte was renowned for smashing her enemies' heads.

God's agenda is for us to turn our fleshly weapons of war into farm implements and agricultural tools—all the better to cultivate the Fruit of the Spirit.

> *He shall judge between the nations, and rebuke many people; they shall beat their swords into plowshares, and their spears into pruning hooks; nation shall not lift up sword against nation, neither shall they learn war anymore.*
>
> Isaiah 2:4 ISV

In God's kingdom, we are kitted out with sevenfold armour for battle. What energises the helmet of salvation, the breastplate of righteousness, the belt of truth, the shoes of the readiness of the gospel of peace, the shield of faith, the sword of the Word and the songs of the Spirit? Is it our faith? Is it the Fruit? No, it's a divine kiss. Simple as that. God sends us out to battle, defended by a kiss. And in our munitions belt, He exhorts us to pack love, joy, peace, patience, kindness, goodness, faithfulness, gentleness and self-control.

He tells us to love our enemies and to do good to those who hate us, to return good for evil. He tells us to honour everyone, not just those who honour us. And He really means *everyone*. It is perilous to dishonour even fallen spirits.

Yet we have a tendency to try to shame anyone we *perceive* has dishonoured us, whether that person has or not. We want vindication of our own honour and we do it by batting back any dishonour or curses aimed at us. We should be returning blessing for blows. We should be taking our orders from Jesus, and inquiring from Him whether to apply love or joy or gentleness as we head for the front line. Instead, we devise a battleplan that seems to have come straight out of a modern military manual that advocates shock-and-awe tactics as well as nuclear retaliation. We're advised:

- To roar at the enemy instead of saying, 'The Lord rebuke you.'
- To charge the adversary's formation as soon as possible, instead of waiting and asking Jesus, 'Is now the appointed time?'
- To think that the more people praying the better because troop numbers matter, instead

of recalling that two or three with Jesus in the midst is all that is needed for victory.

- To assume the authority given to us is the right and the power to bind the enemy, instead of the right and the power to uphold the Word of God. To also assume that '*all* authority' means we are no longer *under* God's authority and that we can make our own rules.

- To break treaties, agreements, and covenants with the enemy that were sworn by our ancestors and that we are bound by, instead of asking God to annul any accords or truces. Jesus has already paid the price for us to rescind these pacts but when we transgress them without going to Him first, we learn what the price written into the agreement was.

- To keep to the recently developed tradition about binding demons,[124] despite there being no recorded instance of Jesus binding any—just rebuking and casting them out.

- To regard as irrelevant the repeated Scriptural injunctions that tell us to restrict ourselves to asking the Lord to rebuke evil and that anything beyond that is dangerous.

- To decree and declare victory instead of preparing the way for it by confessing, repenting, forgiving and renouncing sin.

- To ignore the possibility that the enemy may be allowing us repeated small victories in order to lure us, along with those following us, into a crushing, absolutely devastating trap. The annihilation that follows is a direct result of flouting the repeated warnings of the Holy Spirit.

- To tell the world via social media of all that the Lord has called us to engage in battle-wise—advertising His strategy to both human and spirit enemies, because He's so powerful it doesn't matter. It *does* matter because people can get hurt through such untimely revelations that are more about look-at-me than glorifying God. Prophets who have to be heroes and thereby betray God's counsel set themselves up for God to eventually use them as decoys. Yes, if a prophet continues to leak God's plans in advance, then that prophet will ultimately be used by God to feed the enemy false information.

- To see *peace* in the context of human warfare, not in divine terms. When we do so, we are closer to the Islamic view of faith than we realise. Nabeel Qureshi explains that the description 'religion of peace' only began to emerge as a concept in the 1930s and did not take off until the 1970s. He pointed out that 'Islam' means *surrender* but is related to 'salaam', *peace*. Taken together, he points out that *peace* in this context does not mean an absence of violence, but rather the aftermath of violence.[125] This is entirely different to biblical 'shalom', which is the aftermath of justice, recompense and restitution.[126] Another faith concept that has become more aligned in recent years with Islamic understanding than biblical tenets is prophecy. Today's views are more aligned to fixed fate than to a living word that can be shaped by God in response to changing circumstances and freewill choices and is, moreover, often conditional on our own faithful response.

Our attitude in so much of this is: God's going to rescue us anyway. That's not so if we choose to go our own way.

The problem is not that we don't communicate with God, it's that we don't even try. Like the Israelites feeling buoyed and confident after their victory at Jericho and their snatching back of victory from the jaws of defeat at Ai, we don't bother to ask God when the emissaries of the enemy turn up wanting a covenant with us—a covenant that won't just bind us, but our children and our children's children *forever*.

Communication with God is difficult, make no mistake. Lilith is out there, constantly disrupting our communication lines, distracting us, drawing our attention elsewhere, enhancing big and small frustrations so that we are focussed on fixing them, not on communing and communicating with God. He gives us a strategy to clear those communication lines of interference: singing songs of praise to Him.

As we do so, two things happen: first and most importantly, God comes to inhabit our praises, so we come into direct contact with Him. Secondly, we move beyond the bandwidth of interference caused by the sweet enchantment of demonic singing. We can thus clearly hear God's voice.

All too often we forget that, whatever God has given us to help in the overcoming of the enemy, the enemy will copy in an attempt to counter God's gift. So, of course, there is demonic singing. A choir of sirens—vampiric bird-and-water spirits with voices of enthralling power—constantly attempts to disrupt the communication lines between us and heaven. The scholars who translated the Hebrew Scriptures into Greek in the centuries before Christ chose *sirens* as the closest concept to Lilith. And in the same period, the wives of the Watchers who fathered the human-angelic hybrids, the giant nephilim, were considered to have ultimately become sirens. It's thought that this understanding of them as sirens came from a possible designation as liliths.

Here we see why the ancient Israelite armies were preceded singers and musicians.

> *After consulting the people, the king appointed singers to walk ahead of the army, singing to the Lord and praising Him for His holy splendour. This is what they sang: 'Give thanks to the Lord; His faithful love endures forever!'*
>
> 2 Chronicles 20:21 NLT

Many people today follow the same strategy, unfortunately thinking that the singing is the warfare when, in reality, it's simply a clearing of the air so the Lord's instructions for battle can be heard above the siren song that the enemy uses to confuse us. We're meant to be listening for Him to give us the signal when and how, and even if, to engage the foe.

As well as defensive armour, as well as Fruit that can be used for both protection and attack, as well as songs to counter the disruption of our communication with heaven, God intends for us to have battle companions.

For men, it's necessary to have enough humility to partner with women in the fight against Anat. It's having enough meekness to follow the example of Barak and Jesus, both of whom saw women as essential companions in battle. For men to think that they don't need the help of women is to claim to be better than Jesus—the very same claim that Anat makes. Nothing indicates an alliance with the spirit of dispossession more clearly than such a belief.

Woman was created to be a 'help-meet' to man, to be his armour-bearer and companion for battle in the trials of life. She was designed to be his paraclete—the partner who turns back-to-back with him in the thickest battle and, if he falls, straddles his body in defence and fights on. She is meant to carry him off the field and tend to his wounds.

In reciprocal fashion, he is her paraclete. So he does the same for her if the situation is reversed. This is the Hebrew sense of *submission*—that vexed and misunderstood term that Paul explained in such deep detail when he said, 'Wives, submit to your husbands.' But in our reductionist theology, we compress his lengthy exposition of mutual obligation to five words opposite in intent to his careful explanation. *Submission* in Hebrew is a military term referring to the relationship between a warrior and armour-bearer. It has the sense of *being under* because the armour-bearer is expected to carry the wounded warrior—and vice versa, if necessary. Furthermore the armour-bearer is expected to lift up the other from beneath, so that the warrior can lift up the armour-bearer, so that the armour-bearer can lift up the warrior. Being *under* is not a position of subservience or oppression, it's simply a requirement for *carrying* or *uplifting* another. Paul went to great lengths to spell out his Hebrew understanding of a term he clearly knew could be misunderstood in Greek, but many people ignore his explanation.

That goes for females as well as males. When a woman is complicit with Anat, she can not only fall into the same trap of believing she doesn't need the male—and is therefore also better than Jesus—but, alternatively, she can follow Anat's example of becoming obsessively and unquestionably loyal to her partner, allowing her role as an armour-bearer to devolve into that of a toxic enabler. The position of an armour-bearer requires initiative and boldness—even, at times, the gentle rebuking of some partners to protect them from themselves.

No one should ever offer to another person the kind of trust that should be reserved only for God. This, of course, is true not only in marriage but in groups of any kind—churches, business organisations, voluntary associations, community gatherings, families. Unconditional loyalty in a crisis, particularly during exposure of abuse, can be based in shame—the unbearable shame of having been deceived into investing so much time, effort and financial resource to build the empire of a 'hero' who has proved so untrustworthy. Combined with such shame there's often also intolerable grief that the 'hero' has proved so deeply lacking in integrity—a grief that often gets mired in the first stage of processing, denial.

Men, of course, are often seen as dispossessing women of a potential role as a battle companion. However, the makeup of most organisations being what it is, they dispossess other men much more frequently. Likewise, in my experience, women dispossess other women much more frequently than they do men. In many cases, although we like to attribute misogyny or misandry to the boss, it's often far more personal—it's because we're seen as a threat to their power.[127]

Anat has a multitude of ready excuses in her quiver to fire off, so that those doing the dispossessing can rationalise their actions. In my view, the classic pretext is: *your reaction justifies my action.* Let's tease that out in a specific example: the anger of the person who has been robbed validates the robbery as rightful.

Look at how cause-and-effect is inverted in that scenario. A dispossessor who holds such views is not only narcissistic but is deep in the grip of Egyptian spiritualism—the upside-down, back-to-front, inside-out belief that results in prayers being answered according to the very opposite of our petitions. These narcissists exonerate themselves with the thought that the incandescent fury of the person whose inheritance, birthright, calling or due reward they've appropriated is so wildly unreasonable that it was just as well they didn't get their entitlement. 'Proves I was right,' they think, as they drape their repressed shame in a variant of the mantra, 'I am right.'[128] They did nothing illegal, after all. They don't acknowledge the betrayal. Indeed, the reaction to the betrayal justifies it happening in the first place.

In today's world, we see the victims of crime who fight back being given harsher penalties than their assailants—who sometimes are never arrested in the first place. Anat has the police forces of the western world running scared. They're more concerned with incorrect pronouns than with quelling violent community unrest. Their gentleness and meekness—that should be rightly displayed as strength under control—has deteriorated into mere weakness. Their authority—that should be rightly displayed in upholding the law—has deteriorated into mere powerlessness. But I hesitate to accuse the police themselves. They are, after all, political pawns.

We too are pawns of Anat unless we recognise within ourselves both dispossessed and dispossessor. Even if we've never dispossessed another person, any complicity with Anat means we've dispossessed ourselves. Any agreement with Sheol—any trade of sight for insight, seeing for secrets, vision for knowledge—in any generation needs to be presented to Jesus for annulment. Anat will target our families and friends if we try to revoke that pact on our own authority. She'll dispossess us even more thoroughly than she already has, if we try to go it alone—on the one hand, breaking the truce with her by refusing to trade further with Sheol and, on the other hand, keeping the truce by not involving Jesus.

At the end of the day, it's all about Jesus. He's the one who totally defeated Anat. That's why she's so desperate to keep Him out of the game she plays with us. Because when we are in Him and He is in us, she doesn't have a chance.

One of the issues we face with regard to the shame that Anat makes it so difficult to process is authority.

Nabeel Qureshi wrote: 'Positional authority yields a society that determines right and wrong based on honour and shame. Rational authority creates a society that determines right and wrong based on innocence and guilt.' He went on to say: 'What is "true" in the East is what the authorities tell you. Assessment of truth is through lines of authority, not individual reasoning.'

This is no longer restricted as a general rule to 'the East'. The great social experiment across the western world in the years 2020–2023 was an attempt to shift the very nature of authority in that sphere from *rational* to *positional*.

Qureshi points out: 'When authority is derived from position rather than reason, the act of questioning leadership is dangerous because it has the potential to upset the system. Dissension is reprimanded and obedience is rewarded.' That is precisely what happened during those years and is still ongoing in many places: leaders broke the law, allegedly in the interests of community safety, publicly shaming those who tried to reason with their diktats. Many families were shattered as a result—because many who adhere to *rational authority* simply would not be shamed into obedience. Shame is always ugly but it's particularly suspect when adults are trying to coerce other adults via humiliation rather than humbly engaging in dialogue. Think of the authorities who basically proclaimed: 'I am science' or 'I am your single source of truth' and ask yourself what that says about the nature of their identity.

Because most of us think of God as an autocrat—some of us describing Him as *benevolent*, some of us not so sure about that—we default to believing His authority is positional. That is, dictatorial. Our view of Him is quite double-minded: He's good and loving, of course, but He's also a tyrant. Now, once we actually begin to see that Scripture portrays His rule as one where He repeatedly consults with His council, we realise that it's better described as a democratic kingship. The Head of State doesn't change, but His decrees are tempered by the petitions of those who stand in His council—including human prophets.

We see numerous examples of this when various prophets negotiate with God about the judgment He has passed: Amos, for example, parleys with God and is able to bring about a change of sentence from a locust plague to a plumb line.

Positional authority rests on 'because I say so.' It is capricious. It obeys no higher law than self-serving whim. Rational authority appeals to an external standard—and even God does this. He set up authority in such a way that He is bound by His word and promises, nor can He break His covenant or law. Moreover He indicates His engagement with rational authority rather than positional authority when He says:

> *Come now, and let us reason together, says the Lord: though your sins are as scarlet, they shall be as white as snow; though they are red like crimson, they shall be as wool.*
>
> Isaiah 1:18 NKJV

God doesn't use authority to shame us—He uses His authority to remove shame from us. He has made a covering of righteousness for us, but to avail ourselves of it, we must first accept our guilt and then come into repentance. But of course true repentance means turning to Jesus and asking for His empowerment—and that's all too often where we come unstuck. We're not really sure we want to tear up our truce with Anat with its primary condition of not involving Jesus in the situation. We search for ways of passing over the threshold and into our calling using just our own strength. It takes us a long, long time before we realise it's impossible.

Positional authority demands *submission* in the Greek sense: unquestioned loyalty, silent deference, automatic obedience. Its options are only honour or shame—with no possibility of shame being restored to honour.

Rational authority on the other hand allows for *submission* in the Hebrew sense: mutual uplift, alternation of initiative, challenge of behaviours or decrees. Its options are righteousness and guilt—with a very simple procedure for guilt being returned to righteousness: the grace-gift of repentance.

Positional authority is about hierarchy; rational authority is about relationship. Positional authority is about control; rational authority is about connection. Positional authority is about power and supremacy; rational authority is about meekness and serving one another.

When we take up the authority associated with our calling, we need God's help to choose the right kind.

Prayer

Heavenly Father, thank You for Your blessing of authority given to me to uphold Your laws of love and justice, faithfulness and mercy, peace and humility. I ask Jesus to come as my mediator in this prayer and word it perfectly so that the intention of my heart to seek You, to live in You and You in me, is brought to pass.

Lord, forgive me for the times I have abused Your authority and used it for my own ends.

Thank You for Your gifts of gentleness and meekness to deploy against Anat. Forgive me when I have become like her and allowed strength to be uncontrolled, instead of relying on the humility of Jesus for control. Lord, whether that strength is physical, mental, emotional, spiritual—whether it is willpower or bodypower—I ask Your Holy Spirit to help me pass the tests that will enable the Fruit of gentleness and meekness to mature in me.

Lord, oftentimes I can't hear You. Remind me to sing Your praises at such times and to invite You to inhabit them so that the siren-voices of the enemy are drowned out and the communication lines between You and me are crystal clear.

Lord, Your Word has sometimes been formed into a weapon against me—I forgive those who've questioned my faith, cast doubt on my courage, pressured me into taking steps forward when I sensed Your Holy Spirit saying, 'No, go back.' I repent of believing the lies that were hidden within a wrapping of Your Word. I ask Jesus of Nazareth, by the power of His Cross and resurrection, to give life to the forgiveness and repentance I have just declared so it can achieve all the mending You desire in my life and the lives of others.

Lord, I declare that I dwell in Christ and He dwells in me. I ask You to rebuke and cast out any unholy spirit—any spirit at all but particularly Anat under whatever alias she has used to gain access to me or my family line—that makes a similar claim. It is not I who live, but Christ who lives in me. And I live in Him. I ask Him to annul any agreement, covenant, copyright claim or habitation rights any such unholy spirit has to reside in me or to say that I reside in him or her. I ask Jesus also to forbid any retaliation against me or any of my loved ones or any of the animals I care for or the property You have give me to steward. I also ask Him to make null and void any copies of such agreements and claims. I ask Jesus once again to secure Himself in me as my Cornerstone and to inscribe on my heart the knowledge that, with Him as the precious Foundation of my being, I will never be put to shame.

Lord, draw to me and my Cornerstone the appointed time for me to enter my calling and to fulfil it as You want. Redeem the time so that, however far Anat has pushed the appointed time out into the future, it is brought back into the present. Reverse whatever needs to be reversed so that, like Joshua having extra hours in the day to complete the battle or Hezekiah being given the sign that he will not die but live many extra years, I will have extra days in my lifetime to fulfil Your assignment for me. I also ask for the wisdom not to make mistakes with this grant of extra years.

Where time has been stolen from me or my family, I ask for it to be restored. Where inheritance has been stolen from me or my family, I ask for it to be restored. Where health has been stolen from me or my family, I ask for it to be restored.

I ask that You lead me, gifting me with humility and grace, so that I can share that inheritance wisely and make it a blessing for the nations, for my community, for my family and for myself.

> And I ask all this in and through
> the name of Jesus the Messiah
> and the power of His atoning blood.
> Amen.

5

Threshing Floors

They journeyed a day,
and a second.
After sunrise on the third
the [Rephaim] arrived at the threshing floors ...
... There the name of El revivified the dead,
the blessings of the name of El revivified the heroes.
There rose up Baal Rapiu,
The warriors of Baal and the warriors of Anat.

The Epic of Aqhat, c. 1350 BC

AROUND THE TIME PERIOD of the Judges, an epic poem featuring Anat and various Canaanite divinities described a procedure for bringing the warrior dead back from the grave.[129] It was *The Epic of Aqhat*.

El, whose name revivified the slain, is *not* Yahweh in these texts but Bull El, the leader of the entire pantheon. Baal-Rapiu, *lord of healing*, is a title of Baal-Hadad, the storm-god. The Rephaim are a ghost army who ride to the threshing floor of El, there to be resurrected—their spirits reunited with their restored bodies—after three days.

Long before Jesus rose from the dead,[130] the enemies of God knew enough about His plan of redemption to try to scuttle it and claim it for their own children. To speak for a moment in terms of card-playing, God had declared 'lay-down misère'—as in a game of *Five Hundred*. He was going to win by losing and, moreover, He was going to show His entire hand and let the entire spirit world know just what would happen. The Messiah had to fulfil hundreds of prophecies, stitch back together dozens of major rips in history, recapitulate the tragedies and reshape them to blessings, challenge all the principalities on their own turf and emerge victorious over every one of them.

Now, while *The Epic of Aqhat* had predicted the Rephaim would return to life, Ezekiel had prophesied they would be stopped. After his vision of the Valley of Dry Bones, Ezekiel turns his attention to another valley. Instead of bones returning to life, being joined and enfleshed and breathing again, in the Valley of the Travellers—another name for 'rephaim'—the ride of the ghost warriors to the threshing floor will be brought to a halt.[131] There they will be *muzzled*, though most translations say 'block':

> *On that day I will give to Gog a place for burial in Israel, the Valley of the Travellers, east of the sea. It will* block *the travellers, for there*

> *Gog and all his multitude will be buried. It will be called the Valley of Hamon-gog.*
>
> Ezekiel 39:11 ESV

The word 'muzzle' suggests that it's right at the last moment, when they are on the verge of regaining breath, that their advance is checked.

It may seem strange that these spirits have a threshing floor as their goal. Why would they be interested in a place where, after a harvest, sheaves were laid out and an iron-toothed sledge is run over them, around and around, separating seed from stalk, grain from chaff? Because threshing floors were seen as portals between the material world and the spirit realms. The whole point of a body is to inhabit the physical cosmos—so, to be resurrected, a doorway into it has to be found.

A threshing floor in ancient understanding was not just a place where grain was trodden and later winnowed, it was considered to be a gateway to heaven and to the underworld. Here it was that divination occurred. It was considered an ideal place for people to consult with the deities of the community. They could approach the priestly intermediaries of the gods or goddesses, seeking advice or a knowledge of the future. At these places the veil between heaven and earth was regarded as particularly thin. Tutelary deities could therefore easily witness agreements between humans when they were invoked. Prayer niches were built on threshing floors to honour the gods of fertility. Thus they became preferred places for marriages to be solemnised, for war councils to be held, for judgments to be delivered.

The Tabernacle and the Temple were both associated with threshing floors. Once the Tabernacle had crossed the Jordan, it was stationed, according to the Jewish Board of Deputies, for 14 years at Gilgal, for 369 years at the threshing floor of Shiloh—ignoring, it seems, Shechem and Mizpah[132]—and then for 57 years at Nob and Gibeon[133] before it was parked in the Temple which was built on the threshing floor purchased from Araunah, king of the Jebusites.[134]

The site of the Temple corresponds to Mount Moriah, the place where Abraham was willing to offer up Isaac. Even in Abraham's day, it was probably a threshing floor of the Amorites; the description of a high place surrounded by a thicket corresponds to a threshing floor. Thorn bushes or bramble hedges were planted around them in order to deter wild animals who might be seeking the piles of grain that were often left overnight while waiting for the right wind to begin winnowing.[135]

Mount Moriah may simply have originally meant *mountain of the Amorites* and been a locality that served as a portal to the godlings of the Canaanites. Abraham went there, as I have argued at length in *Dealing with Kronos*, not because Yahweh asked him to sacrifice his son but because 'ha'elohim'—*the angels*—did. Yahweh stopped the test, but I do not believe He initiated it. It's my view that 'ha'elohim' always means *the angels* or *the heavenly ones*, while 'elohim' can mean either *God* or the *angels*.

Another place that may well have been a threshing floor is Bethel where Jacob had the dream of angels ascending and descending a ladder. People who were, for whatever reason, unwilling to seek shelter in a town overnight would have found threshing floors with their defensive thickets a place of protection against wild animals.

Threshing floors were seen as places open to heaven. But that didn't mean that the communication lines were restricted to Yahweh. I used to be completely baffled by Isaiah's poem about the Precious Cornerstone to be laid in Zion. I couldn't make any sense of the abrupt and seemingly random transition from the necessity of annulling covenants with Death and with Sheol to God's design for agriculture:

> *Grain must be ground to make bread; so one does not go on threshing it forever. The wheels of a threshing cart may be rolled over it, but one does not use horses to grind grain. All this also comes from the Lord Almighty, whose plan is wonderful, whose wisdom is magnificent.*
>
> Isaiah 28:28-29 NIV

And then, when I realised two immensely significant things, it became clear that this isn't a haphazard change of topic at all. First important point: this is a description of a threshing floor and, generally speaking, threshing floors are round. Second important point: you don't stomp repeatedly on the spot to separate grain, you go around and around and around. And around and around and around. And around.

Like Jericho. I wonder if the people of Jericho looked out on the Israelites circling their city and thought to themselves with dread, 'They're threshing us. Threshing. They're opening a doorway for their God to sweep down and blow this town away like chaff.'

Now even before Jericho, the Israelites had been thinking in circles. They'd been camped at Gilgal where they'd renewed their covenant with God through the sign of circumcision and had set up twelve stones. Gilgal means *wheel* or *circle of stones*.

In past centuries, *gilgal* was an English word, derived from Hebrew, for structures like Stonehenge. In more recent times, it has become the name for the archaeological discoveries of giant footsteps surrounded by stone-edged pathways that are dotted along the Jordan Valley. Within the outline of the foot are places for altars and, in some locations, there are tiers where the people could look down on the ceremonies. It appears that the pathways were for worshippers to go around and around and around the altar, singing praises and dancing for joy in the Lord's presence.

When we read that the first site of the Tabernacle was

at Gilgal for 14 years, we naturally think of the Gilgal near Jericho. However, that may not be the case. There is another Gilgal mentioned in Deuteronomy 11:30 where the Israelites were directed to go on entering the land. It was near the Trees of Moreh in the vicinity of Mount Gerizim and Mount Ebal.[136]

In fact, just such a sanctuary in the shape of a footprint has been found at Mount Ebal. This was where Joshua twice led the people in reaffirmation of the covenant with God. His first ceremony of reaffirmation was at another Gilgal, the one near Jericho, when the rite of circumcision took place. The reference by Moses to the Gilgal at the Trees of Moreh is one of those passages that simply exudes first-hand knowledge of the locality and seems to suggest that he's been there, remembers it and has described it repeatedly to the people so they recognise it when they get where they should be going.

And if all this is so, then before the Israelites adopted a threshing floor as their preferred site for the Tabernacle and Temple, the original form was a sacred precinct shaped like a foot that people circled as they sang to the Lord and sacrificed and celebrated in His presence.

The foot was a multi-layered symbol.

- It spoke of inheritance, since God had promised Joshua:

    'I will give you every place where you set your foot.'

Joshua 1:3 NIV

- It spoke of God's footstool.

  This is what the Lord says: 'Heaven is My throne, and the earth is My footstool. Where is the house that you would build for Me, and where will My resting place be?'

  Isaiah 66:1 ISV

- It spoke of God walking the land. Six similar structures have been found so far, though none yet near Jericho. Such giant steps are an image of God traversing the landscape and therefore declare His ownership of it. Three of these footprints have been found in the Jordan Valley, all oriented towards Adam, the ancient locality that marked the limit of the waters of the river receding during the crossing of the Jordan after the years of wilderness wandering.

Now it seems to me that a threshing floor is a convenient substitute for a gilgal. One is multi-purpose, one reserved for sacred ceremonies. One is surrounded by a protective thicket; one by low walls of stones with a pathway between. One is set in a high place to catch the wind; one was built on a flat area below a nearby slope. One requires minimal maintenance; one requires regular upkeep. One can be used as is; one has to be carefully crafted with a specific orientation. One is set up for the privacy of the priests; one is built so an audience can sit on a slope and watch the singers and the priests.[137] Their common feature is that they are both designed to be circled.

The multiplicity of these structures suggests that there was no singular place where God was thought to reside; no especially 'holy' venue where the people were called to assemble at the times of 'mo'ed'—*the appointed feasts* of the Lord. It was unnecessary to travel even to the Tabernacle to approach God—the local gilgal would be fine. This idea must have persisted long past the time when the Tabernacle was moved to Shiloh because Saul, the first king of Israel, was proclaimed at Gilgal near Mizpah during what was obviously a 'mo'ed' since all the tribes had gathered there.

Now the word, 'mo'ed', is often translated *appointed time* but its nuances are entirely different from 'kairos' or 'eth' as *appointed time* with their sense of a moment of opportunity that can be seized by ritual sacrifice. Certainly 'mo'ed' is associated with sacrifice but it is for a return to right relationship and standing with God, not for snatching a fortuitous chance.

Gilgals were the very opposite of 'high places' where the Canaanites worshipped their deities. Threshing floors, on the other hand, were the very same 'high places' where the Canaanites worshipped their deities.

So, in all this, a question arises: was the use of a threshing floor for the sacred foundations at Shiloh and Jerusalem yet another time when God accommodated Himself to our human desire to have our own way? God didn't want His people to have a king, but they insisted, so He not only granted it but blessed the institution. God didn't ask for a static Temple but He agreed to it, eventually descending in glory to set His name there. There were many times God did not look with favour on that Temple or on its rebuilding, but He honoured those who came in humility and contrite repentance.[138]

When we seek convenience rather than God's timing, we are looking for an appointed time to suit ourselves. We want opportunity to arrive when we're ready, not before or after. And when we sacrifice others, as we often do, on the altar of our own convenience we have fallen into the net Anat has laid right at the doorway to the treasury of restored inheritance. Convenience can all too easily become an idol tucked away at the back of a false refuge and hidden inside it, like a nesting doll.

'I am an inconvenience.'

I am deeply grateful to the man who had the courage to struggle with his shame to the point where he could articulate these words. It's not quite the same as *'I am wrong'* but it's close. Getting in touch with shame is difficult enough without the additional burden of trying to tease out the exact statement that expresses it. Most people begin to shut down their emotions long before they can get anywhere near this stage.

Naturally, this is an identity belief. It's an 'I am' statement. It's not that I do inconvenient things, though of course that happens too. It's that I am, in the very essence of my being, an inconvenience. This belief was instilled in the man even before he was born: the baby growing in the womb was coming at an inconvenient time for the parents. His birth was inconvenient for his parents and it was all too easy for them to slide into treating him as inconvenient. And for that behaviour to set the pattern for all of life.

Shame, disappointment, unreadiness for an appointed time and self-rejection are all wrapped up in these four simple words: *I am an inconvenience.*

Therefore everything I do will be inconvenient. As a result, I will be shamed. I will be a disappointment to myself and others. My shame and self-rejection will intensify. I hesitate as I approach appointments because I'm aware something always goes wrong—circumstances that once were favourable now seem to conspire against me, and I'm unprepared for the moment because I'm suddenly juggling so many troubles that need to be sorted. The appointment is no longer convenient; it's a problem.

'I am an inconvenience' encapsulates an acceptance of dishonour as a layer over a foundation of shame and the core belief: *I did not come into the world at the appointed time*. This plays straight into Anat's hands from birth, if not conception. It can go further and say to us: *wrong time, wrong place, wrong family, wrong me*.

At its most basic, it's a belief that enables her to push out the true appointed time for our calling ever further into the future—until it is beyond our own lifetime. It also enables her to plunge us, ever so slowly and subtly, into the quicksand of Egyptian spiritualism—so we receive from the Lord the opposite of what we prayed for. It may also result in us shutting down our prophetic gift: because our prayers seem to be so out of alignment with what comes to pass.

Sometimes, of course, there are other reasons for shutting down the prophetic gift, especially if it's done early in life. When we sense the relentless pressure of Sheol to exchange sight for knowledge—and we are, rightly, afraid of the trade, and further we realise our 'no' is not being taken as 'no' but simply as an invitation to exert more intense pressure—we may decide to remove the gift from our lives. If we have nothing that Sheol wants, then it won't bother us anymore. That's our thinking. So we switch off God's gift to us, bury it, or somehow give it away.

But that's not the answer. We are indeed born for such a time as this. The person we are most inconvenient to is Anat, so she expends enormous energy to convince us that we are the inconvenience. And so we are. The reason we believe her is because it's true. We are an inconvenience to *her*. And the closer we come to God and the more we step into the calling He has for us, then the more inconvenient we'll become, and the bigger threat we'll pose. To *her*.

But not to God.

When we regain our inheritance, we'll be dispossessing her as the dispossessor. So we need to ask Jesus to remove the impediments in the way of the return of our inheritance. We need to ask Him to annul our covenant with Death and our agreements with Sheol, to replace the cornerstone of our lives with Himself as the Chief Cornerstone, and to bring us to God's gilgal and threshing floor.

The prophet Isaiah tells us that, when the true and precious cornerstone is laid in Zion and the covenants with Death and Sheol are cancelled, then the Lord will teach us appropriate measures for a gilgal where threshing takes place.

> *The wheels of a threshing cart may be rolled* [gilgal] *over it, but one does not use horses to grind grain. All this also comes from the Lord Almighty, whose plan is wonderful, whose wisdom is magnificent.*
>
> Isaiah 28:28–29 NIV

This is such an unusual use of 'gilgal' that Isaiah seems to be hinting at the return to a more ancient ceremony: a time of joyous circling, of dancing in delight during an assembly at a divinely appointed time. Perhaps he was prophesying about Simchat Torah, *rejoicing in the Torah*, the separate and extra day that God added to the week-long Feast of Tabernacles and that has become, in modern times, associated with the ending and beginning of the readings in the Torah cycle.

It was on Simchat Torah in 2023 that Hamas broke through, and paraglided over, the Gaza border, slaughtering over 1200 civilians and kidnapping hundreds of hostages. Many of those abducted were taken from a dance festival where revellers circled a silver buddha. A counterfeit gilgal during the very time corresponding in the ancient calendar to Anat's worship at Ra'shu Yeni completely forfeits God's protection. It's little different to those leaders in Jerusalem during the time of Isaiah who were practising necromancy and bargaining with the underworld in an effort to ward off the Assyrian invasion.

Yet Hezekiah and his court officials repented—and were granted a spectacular miracle involving both a time reversal and the complete annihilation of an invading army. We too can repent and be brought back, as Hezekiah was, from the brink of death and destruction.

On 31 January, 2020, *Pengbai*—China's state-run news outlet—reported that 'People's Liberation Army Major General Chen Wei, took over the response to the epidemic,' including supervision of the Wuhan Institute of Virology. *Pengbai* described Dr Chen as the head of biological warfare division at the Academy of Military Medical Sciences. A virologist, the general was dubbed 'our nation's ultimate expert' in biological and chemical weapon defences, and 'a goddess of war'. Her other nickname is the 'Wolf Warrior'.[139]

A goddess of war? It won't take a mind-reader to know what I'm thinking at this point. Hmm... *spike* proteins, *bat* coronaviruses,[140] jabs, shots, needles, injections—I wonder what war goddess those words remind us of.

Now a month previously, Chinese authorities were treating dozens of cases in Wuhan of the coronavirus that would eventually become known as COVID-19. However, it was still six weeks before the World Health Organisation would declare a pandemic and much of the world would decide to lockdown for two weeks to 'flatten the curve.' Soon we were in the midst of the longest two weeks in history.

And then we were rescued—by a vaccine. Never mind that the definition of 'vaccine' was quietly modified to include gene therapy so that most people's trust in the long history of vaccines could be used to advantage. Never mind that anyone who was listening carefully and noticed the contradictions, often between one sentence and the next, was cautious. Or that there were those mindful of John Stuart Mill's axiom, 'All silencing of discussion is an assumption of infallibility.'

Instead of rational discourse, instead of persuasive dialogue by the infallible ones, there was—on both sides—shaming, coercion, domination, manipulation and control. At other times, discerning believers would have recognised these instantly as the tools of witchcraft, but suddenly that was okay if they were keeping us safe.

One thing I've learned in my years of studying thresholds is this: beware the same wording. When people use exactly and precisely the same words every time when talking about a situation, then unless they are actually quoting, they are almost certainly hiding relevant details. Truth can be expressed in many different ways, but when someone is trying to avoid outright lying but still conceal awkward aspects of a matter, they keep to a very narrow set of words and phrases. So by the time I'd heard 'safe and effective' for the thousandth time, I looked up the definition. 'Safe and effective' in medical terminology back in 2020 meant this: if a person is given a treatment at the right time, under the right conditions, in the right amount, and it is rightly administered, there being no contra-indications, *then the benefits outweigh the risks.* Who could have guessed that 'safe and effective' actually had an inbuilt condition about 'right timing' and thus appointed time?

Another thing I've learned the hard way is this; in fact, I've been dispossessed in the process of learning it: when assessing the relative merits of disputed matters, it's wise to be far more suspicious about the argument of those who have something to gain, and far less suspicious about those who have something to lose. And when it comes right down to it, as a general rule, truth almost always resides with those who have everything to lose by taking the stance they do.

Now it's political suicide for any of our leaders to admit they were wrong. That's a fact even if they aren't narcissists who hold to the mantra, 'I am right.' But let's face it, the contents of the vaccine aside, the plain evidence of the hallmarks of Lilith—bats, spikes and jabs—and the symbols of Anat—war goddess, violence and threats of violence, extreme coercion and total abuse of the rule of law as well as human rights legislation—says it all. It was her time to arise and she hasn't finished yet.

Let me also say this. From the start, there was considerable question as to whether mRNA shots could modify DNA. We were assured and reassured it could not happen. Some people still maintain that's the case but they're dwindling in number. As far as I am concerned, if there is even the tiniest, most remote possibility that DNA can be altered, it's a closed case. That's my position even before I take into account that production involves centrifugal action, the round-and-round whirling of threshing matter.[141]

With DNA alteration, we'd be back in the days of the Watchers who deliberately planned to mate with human women, thus altering the genetic lines descending from them so they were no longer quite human. The Watchers plotted to destroy God's redemptive plan and nullify His promise to Adam and Eve. Only God's intervention in bringing down a worldwide flood kept it on track.

We cannot take the risk of repeating the sin of transgressing the species boundary. This is specifically addressed in Jude 1:6 and requires repentance. So, if you have a sense that you've made a mistake and believed authorities you no longer trust, don't start to shut down because of shame. Don't close off and wrap yourself in denial. Ask the Lord to turn your shame into guilt and then deal with it through repentance and the life-giving empowerment of the blood of Jesus. And then ask Him to fix your DNA and restore it to its right design. Sound and song will be integral to that mending.

Now Jude indicates that the Watchers were bound in chains, awaiting God's final judgment. But he does not mention the fate of the wives of the Watchers. In texts outside the Bible, they are said to have become *sirens* or *liliths*.

David Kupelian relates a haunting story told to him by his grandmother about the Armenian genocide and the strange forces that controlled the Muslim Turks. 'They were very hospitable and would invite you in,' she said. 'But, if a distant signal was given—it sounded something like a trumpet—then they would instantly change, and would attempt to harm you. Yet if the signal sounded again, they would immediately switch back to normal. Even if they had injured you after the first signal, as soon as the second signal sounded, they would bind up the very wounds they had inflicted on you.'

Even as a small boy Kupelian found it a very strange tale, with overtones of *The Manchurian Candidate* and post-hypnotic suggestion triggering murderous, pre-programmed behaviour. Kupelian mentioned this story to a colleague and was put in touch with Islam scholar Andrew Bostom who confirmed it from several sources. One of these was a *New York Times* story from 25 September, 1915, quoting Dr. M. Simbad Gabriel, head of a U.S.-based Armenian organisation: 'When the bugle blows in the morning, Turks rush fiercely to the work of killing the Christians and plundering them of their wealth. When it stops in the evening, or in two or three days, the shooting and stabbing stop just as suddenly then as it began. The people obey their orders like soldiers.'

Bostom revealed he'd read accounts of 'a call to arms where Muslims would show up at residences— people who lived with neighbours for a decade or more—and engaged in indiscriminate slaughter.'[142]

Similarly, in *Farewell, Babylon: Coming of Age in Jewish Baghdad*, Naim Kattan speaks of a community that had existed from the time of Nebuchadnezzar and had lived amicably with their neighbours—Christian or Muslim—for centuries. They had engaged in intellectual and social debate in homes and meeting places, thought of themselves as Iraqis, all united against a common enemy: the hated English. And then came the *Farhoud*, a sudden genocidal eruption of violence by the Muslims in the few days of transition between the leaving of the Germans, after the British victory in the Anglo-Iraqi war, and the return of the young king from Iran.

The strangeness in many of these stories is, for me, the reversion to normality after two or three days. That is reminiscent of the Nazi 'aktion' campaigns against the Jews and other minority groups that would last a similar length of time, then stop, only to be repeated again some weeks later. For many years I wondered why the first campaign simply didn't keep on going until it achieved complete eradication of the target group. I've come to two conclusions: first, it's about build-up of terror and, secondly and probably the most significantly, I don't think it is possible for it to continue indefinitely without the programming falling apart. The human mind needs a break in the killing or it will break.

We can see various tactics peculiar to Anat in these stories: triggering sounds, appointed times that cannot be extended, short bursts of extreme violence targeting peaceable civilian neighbours. Her contribution to warfare is different from that of her foremost ally, Kronos-Belial, the spirit of abuse. His is more regimented and involves the kind of mind control that operates by taking children and bringing them up to war against their parents: the concept of the Janissary.[143] A key tenet of the spirit behind the Janissary is that the enemy will resource the war against themselves. That is, parents will unknowingly support those who want to take their children from them; voters will elect those who want to do away with democracy; donors will give towards the promotion of trafficking in the belief that they are assisting to eradicate it; the military will leave behind entire arsenals of usable weapons as they withdraw from a war zone.

Clearly, if it's possible to stop the triggering signal, then Anat's strategy falls apart. We therefore have to change or disrupt the sound. The answer is simple. It's already given to us right at the beginning of the spiritual warfare passage that culminates in the Armour of God:

> *Be filled with the Spirit, speaking to one another with psalms, hymns, and songs from the Spirit. Sing and make music from your heart to the Lord, always giving thanks to God*

the Father for everything, in the name of our Lord Jesus Christ.

Ephesians 5:18–20 NIV

Listen for the Lord's song as He takes great delight in you, singing and blessing and rejoicing over you.[144] Join with Him to make a symphony of sound.

In that day,

the Lord will punish with His sword—his fierce, great and powerful sword—Leviathan the gliding serpent, Leviathan the coiling serpent; He will slay the monster of the sea.

In that day—

'Sing about a fruitful vineyard: I, the Lord, watch over it; I water it continually. I guard it day and night so that no one may harm it. I am not angry. If only there were briers and thorns confronting Me! I would march against them in battle; I would set them all on fire. Or else let them come to Me for refuge; let them make peace with Me, yes, let them make peace with Me.'

In days to come Jacob will take root, Israel will bud and blossom and fill all the world with fruit.

Isaiah 27:1–6 NIV

Here Isaiah connects two aspects of the Day of the Lord: the slaying of Leviathan and the Lord's song over a vineyard—the symbol of inheritance. God expresses His disappointment, lamenting that His chosen people do not seek refuge in Him. Nor are they simple thorns to be eliminated by battle or burning. That's a strange thought, but it connects directly to the next chapter's warning regarding false refuges, and covenants with Death and Sheol.

As we've seen, an agreement with Sheol involves Lilith, whose symbols include stakes, spears, stabs, jabs, thorns, talons. Thorns are mentioned here and the particular word for them, used only seven times in Scripture and always by Isaiah, is thought to derive from *to set* or *appoint*. Again, this is about *appointed time*. Of course. What else is the Day of the Lord, except an appointed time?

The importance of singing over an inheritance is also highlighted. We are called to renounce our false refuges and our agreements with Death and Sheol and join the Lord in His song.

He wants to break the chains over us. Though, when it comes to Lilith, it's more accurate to describe the chains as a 'net' to go with her weapon, the spear. Think of those gladiators armed with a trident or a spear and a net: that's a picture of her opposition to us.

Generally speaking, the spear takes us out and we spend years, transfixed by trauma to a moment in the past. But then, finally, it dawns on us to ask Jesus to deal with the spear and all its barbs. Once we're free, we're not likely to be caught like that again. We'll head straight to our Paraclete Jesus to get the wound dressed and the blade removed.

So Lilith changes tactic. A harpoon is just like a spear but with a rope attached.[145] It's a similar trauma but we're not stuck anymore, so perhaps we won't notice the harpoon slowing us down. Once we feel utterly exhausted, the rope begins to slowly pull us back. Yet again, we're moving away from the appointed time, until it finally dawns on us what the problem is. So we ask our Paraclete Jesus to remove the harpoon and its hooks, and tend our wound.

Lilith engages in another alteration of tactics. She takes up a magic net and enlists those who have never renounced their agreements with Sheol:

> *And now, Son of Man, turn toward and oppose the women of your people who prophesy according to their own wrong inclinations and prophesy against them. Tell them, 'This is what the Lord God says, "How terrible it will be for those women who sew magical bracelets on all their wrists and make one-size-fits all headbands, in order to entrap their souls. Will you hunt for the souls of my people and remain alive? You've profaned me among my people for a handful of barley and a morsel of bread. You're causing people to die who shouldn't have to die, and you're causing*

people to live who shouldn't survive, when you deceive my people who tend to listen to lies."'

Therefore, this is what the Lord God says, 'Watch out! I'm opposing your amulets with which you hunt souls as one would swat at a flying insect. I'll tear them off your arms and then deliver those people, whom you've hunted like birds.'

Ezekiel 13:17–20 ISV

Five women prophets are named in the Hebrew portion of the Scriptures—Miriam, Deborah, Huldah, Noadiah and 'the prophetess' married to Isaiah. However there was also a guild of women prophets from the time of Ezekiel. He mentions them in this appalling denunciation where they use 'magical bracelets' to trap souls and thus bargain with Sheol for who will live and who will die.

The word translated *magical bracelet* is 'kesheth', found here and nowhere else in Scripture, and variously rendered as *magic charm, pillow, band* or *filet*. My view is that *filet* is the most accurate term as it describes *knotted net lace*. I consider that 'kesheth' is a poetical combination of 'resheth', *net*, from *inherit* or *dispossess*, and 'kesheph', *sorcery*.

These women hunt souls by telling convincing lies. They are masters of propaganda. They lure people into their net, just as sirens do with their singing. They prophesy with charming words that are always positive and that never call for repentance or forgiveness, for renouncing ties with darkness and Death, Sheol and Lilith, or any of the other threshold spirits.

This magic net of disinheritance and dispossession entangles us so tightly it is much worse than the bonds of a threefold cord. We can identify line after line and ask Jesus to cut them, but still not get free. We need to inquire of the Holy Spirit what the lines are made of and to direct us to a group of knots close together so that the lines in the same area can all be severed. We don't necessarily need the whole net gone, just a big hole in it so the hand of Jesus can pull us through. He is the only one who can release us from this stranglehold of the enemy and bring us safe to the stronghold of God.

Prayer

Heavenly Father, thank You that, no matter what the enemy plans, no matter how impassable the blockade in my way, how deep the pit, how subtle the snare, how tight the net, how jagged and poison-tipped the spear, how explosive the harpoon, how long my imprisonment, Your marvellous breakthrough is still ready and waiting for me.

Please help me to fulfil all the necessary conditions for its activation: forgiveness, repentance, removal of false refuges, renunciation of unholy vows and dark covenants, lifting of dishonour, dissolution of agreements with the lies of the enemy, undoing of my unbelief in the atonement and of my reliance on formulaic approaches to You instead of Jesus.

Please whisk me off to Your Holy Spirit hospital to treat all the wounds I've been subjected to. Please remove the spears, knives, lances, thorns and injections, along with the poisons they carried, and the trauma they brought to my body, mind, heart, soul and spirit. Where they changed the essential 'me' in some way, sing me into wholeness and bring me into harmony with the design You've always intended for me. Show me what the net used to entrap me is made of, so I can do my part to ready myself for the moment You cut open a hole to bring me out.

Empower me through the blood of Jesus, shed for love of all the world, to be gentle, meek and humble of heart.

Teach me the song You're singing over me and over my inheritance so I can sing along with You. Keep me in constant communication with You and, when the heavenly bandwidth is distorted so I cannot hear Your Holy Spirit, remind me that You inhabit the praises of Your people. So inspire me to speak Your praise and read Your praise and declare Your praise and sing Your praise and to give You constant thanksgiving for the blessings and favour You shower into my life.

> In the wonderful Name of Jesus of Nazareth.
> Amen.

6

Jesus, Just Jesus

*The Spirit of the Lord shall rest upon him—
the Spirit of wisdom and understanding,
the Spirit of counsel and might,
the Spirit of knowledge and of the fear of the Lord.*

Isaiah 11:2 NKJV

ANAT'S GREEK EQUIVALENT ATHENA, a goddess of warfare, also offers wisdom, understanding, knowledge, counsel and might. But not, of course, the fear of the Lord God. In fact, her counterfeit system is to replace the fear of the Lord with fear of Anat. Like her Egyptian counterpart Neith, *the terrifying one*, she makes us afraid. Bowel-loosening, heart-stopping, brain-freezing-petrified. Such fear is a matter for shame and thus needs to be covered up. The dread is so humiliating we can't even admit to the terror she evokes. We hide it from ourselves in an iron-clad denial system.

Men, in particular, interpret shame as failure and weakness. The fear of failure is really a fear of shame and ridicule. They fear showing fear. They can take the loss but not the shame that comes with the loss. Anger and withdrawal are the result. Think Elijah's retreat to the Mountain of God and the collapse of his calling.

Anat will try unceasingly to deflect us away from Jesus. Of course, she doesn't want us to realise this. Elijah could get to the mountain, speak to God Himself, and yet still be so influenced by terror of her that God's words did not really penetrate.

Anat is a rival to Jesus. Yet she doesn't so much want to rule heaven, as she wants to decide who does. Claiming, like Neith, to be the judge of the gods, she won't render any verdict that goes against her favourite. And Jesus isn't in that position. She wants Him out of the picture. He's the only one who threatens her power but she arouses so much dread in us that she seems to threaten His. She claims both creation and re-creation, that is, resurrection, are hers to dispense as she sees fit.

Anat's Greek counterpart, Athena, was said to have woven all of the world and existence into being on her loom.[146] Anat's brother Baal was said to have known the word of nature, that is, the word that when spoken authoritatively will result in creation but he will only reveal that word to Anat in the sanctuary on Zaphon.[147] Furthermore Anat claims to have the ability to give people life.[148] All of this is counter to Jesus as the Word of God, the Creator and the Word made flesh.

Now we may not be confused about Jesus and Anat, but many of us are completely confused about the Father and Anat. This is not a modern problem. In fact, at one time in Egypt—*where else?*—Yahweh and Anat were combined into a single entity, Yaho-Anat. But it's not a problem that can be relegated to the past, either. When we mentally separate the Persons of the Trinity and think of the Father as an ancient white-haired figure whose vengeful 'Old Testament' guise was tempered by gentle 'New Testament' Jesus, then we come perilously close to imaging the Father as Anat. This completely undermines our ability to trust Him.

So, out of fear of Anat, and out of lack of trust that Jesus will protect us from her, too many of us have agreed to a truce. That's what I've discovered in prayer counselling. The cease-fire is so prevalent that I suspect it is nearly universal. Not everyone is aware of the existence of this truce. In fact, very few people are. But one invariable condition in it is this: *leave Jesus out of this. We can resolve our differences without His input.*

Consequently, the most obvious sign of such a truce is a reluctance to use the name of Jesus in prayer. There are whole groups of believers who avoid identifying Him by name, instead calling Him the 'Omnipotence', the 'Power' or the 'Higher Power'. Now this is ambiguous: not only does Anat, in my view, belong to the group in the spiritual hierarchy called the 'exousias', *powers*, she claims that her power is the superior one. Just like reducing Belial to the description, *worthless*, this is reducing Jesus to the description, *power*.

However there are also other signs, such as singing half a dozen 'worship' songs but never mentioning His name; looking to those with gifts of prophecy for an encouraging word instead of getting hope directly from the Holy Spirit. And of course there's the other signs I've noted previously: going out into the street and using the power of Jesus to heal people but never mentioning Him; or writing books where faith is reduced to an absence of immorality and where not even the slightest hint of Christianity is apparent; or using our own 'positional' authority to decree or declare a desired and convenient outcome.

We're expert at rationalising the reasons we nudge aside the Name above all names and exclude Jesus from the public arena. But the bottom line is: lack of trust in Him as our covenant defender. This is a lack of trust we have no means of overcoming unless we trust Him—and that's the very thing we can't do. Remember the net of Lilith? Sometimes we've deliberately tangled ourselves in it, thinking of it as a safety net not as a snare. In our minds, we say to God, 'Get me out!' but at the same time, our hearts are demanding, 'Leave me alone!'

It took me over twenty years to realise I was double-minded about the double-bind in my life. I'd pray regularly, saying to God, 'When I have the money to do what I believe is Your will for my life, I don't have the time. When I have the time, I don't have the money. I need You to sort this for me.'

Eventually God said to me one day, 'You know why I haven't answered that prayer? You don't want Me to.'

After my initial shock, I searched my heart for some time and realised God was right. The very thought of the double-bind being gone was enough to edge me towards panic-stricken shutdown. I was comfortable where I was, but just the prospect of one step further was totally unnerving. I realised that I'd reached the limit of my trust in God decades ago, and nothing had changed in all the intervening years.

So I said to the Lord after a few weeks of reflection on the relatively secure nature of camping on the edge of the wilderness and going neither forward nor backward, 'You know, I don't think I'll go on. I've been here a long time and realised it's ok here. It's a lot like Elijah's situation after he spoke to You at Horeb. You gave him a task and he didn't fulfil it. But You were kind to Elijah, You even took him to heaven in a whirlwind. You haven't changed. You'll be just as kind to me.'

It was one of those times when the voice of God was exceptionally clear. 'But you,' He said, 'are not like Elijah. You are like Ahaz.'

'No!' I couldn't think of anything more horrifying. It was like a body-blow. 'Anyone but Ahaz!' Suddenly I had massive incentive to get rid of the double-bind.

Ahaz is the king of Judah who received the prophecy of Immanuel. That was to be God's sign to him that the alliance of powers lining up against him would be destroyed.

> *Again the Lord spoke to Ahaz: 'Ask a sign of the Lord your God; let it be deep as Sheol or high as heaven.'*
>
> *But Ahaz said, 'I will not ask, and I will not put the Lord to the test.'*
>
> *And he [Isaiah] said, 'Hear then, O house of David! Is it too little for you to weary men, that you weary my God also? Therefore the Lord Himself will give you a sign. Behold, the virgin shall conceive and bear a son, and shall call his name Immanuel. He shall eat curds and honey when he knows how to refuse the evil and choose the good. For before the boy knows how to refuse the evil and choose the good, the land whose two kings you dread will be deserted.'*
>
> Isaiah 7:10–16 ESV

It's clear this prophecy was meant to be fulfilled within a very few years. It wasn't meant to delay seven centuries. Nor was the alliance Ahaz feared meant to attack and devastate the country, as they did. So how did Isaiah get it so wrong?

Prophecy is not fixed fate. If it were, the threshold guardians would know exactly how to maximise the damage and demolish it. Every time they blockade us totally, God allows for re-interpretation so the prophecy can still be fulfilled. Prophecy is not set in stone but planted in time. It's organic, flexible, capable of regrowing even when it's been entirely cut down.

Isaiah's prophecy was not inaccurate, but it was still subject to the freewill choices of Ahaz. And Ahaz determined to destroy the promised sign. According to many Jewish commentators, Immanuel is the son described here as an offering to the fire-god Moloch:

He [Ahaz] *even sacrificed his own son as a burnt offering to idols, imitating the disgusting practice of the people whom the Lord had driven out of the land.*

2 Kings 16:3 GNT

Jesus, as the fulfilment of Isaiah's prophecy, is the Second Immanuel, just as He is the Second Adam, the Second Moses, the Second Joshua, the Second Samson, the Second Elijah, the Second Elisha. So you see why I was horrified when God compared me to Ahaz. By refusing to do anything about my double-bind, I'd be like someone who not only despised God's sign, created especially for me, but was also willing to defile and destroy it by handing it over as an offering to God's enemies.

So I basically told God I was incapable of even wanting to do anything about the double-bind. Therefore He'd have to undo it for me. Realising the very idea engendered panic, I told Him He could ignore any attempts to withdraw the permission I was giving Him to do whatever needed to be done. It didn't matter how much I kicked and screamed and asked Him to stop, He had my full permission to disregard my tantrums.

This may seem strange. But God never violates free will. If He did, He'd be an abuser. So we have to give Him the rights to override any withdrawal of permission on our part.

It was a good thing I did so. The panic was extreme. And it continued for three days. Even when I asked His help, the panic only moderated slightly before rising again. Then it was over. The double-bind was gone. And I wondered why I'd waited twenty years to feel such enormous release.

During those twenty years, I thought God was teaching me patience. But that, like so many other excuses, was simply covering up the pit of fear. A fear I didn't even know existed. Yet once God had pointed out the double-bind to me, I realised that deep within was a sense that something had a claim on me. I was supposed to be the Temple of the Holy Spirit but I realised my false refuges with their secret shrines meant I was more like the Temple in Ezekiel's time with its hidden rooms decorated with idols. And because of that unconscious idolatry, I wasn't completely sure Jesus would protect me. It wasn't just that my Temple building was wrong, it went right back to my cornerstone, the very first cell of my being. I'm like David:

> *Surely I was sinful at birth, sinful from the time my mother conceived me.*
>
> Psalm 51:5 NIV

But there's good news. I am a place as well as a person. So what applies to a place also applies to me. Isaiah's prophecy about the new Cornerstone is as much for me as it is for Jerusalem. But it turns out to be only half the story. There's another aspect that needs to be there: the Cloud.

Together the Cornerstone and the Cloud form the protective covering of God. In addition to His armour and the Fruit He's provided as weapons for our defence, He adds in covering that kicks in at the appointed time.

Now the Cornerstone and the Cloud are constantly linked throughout Scripture. They are associated with two special 'mo'edim', *appointed times:* Yom Kippur and Sukkot. These were set times for festivals, and should not to be confused with the fleeting appointed times for grasping hold of opportunity.

Yom Kippur: Day of Atonement.
Sukkot: Feast of Tabernacles.

These assemblies were six days apart. It was during Tabernacles that Jesus began His ministry at Cana. As we've seen, this was the feast of Ra'shu Yeni, *first wine*, in the Canaanite calendar and a time to commemorate the gore-fests of Anat.

Three years later during Tabernacles, Jesus ascended the Mount of Assembly into the war council of the gods. There He was transfigured as a Cloud descended while a Voice proclaimed, *'This is My beloved son.'*

This is the moment when the presence of the Cloud became explicit. The Cornerstone had made its appearance six days before this dazzling revelation of Jesus' glory. At that earlier time, Jesus had been at Caesarea Philippi. It was Yom Kippur. Back in Jerusalem, the high priest would have been casting lots to see which of two goats would be sacrificed and which sent off as the scapegoat to the goat-demon Azazel in the wilderness. And there was Jesus out in the wilderness imaging Himself as the scapegoat as He stood outside the Gates of Hell at the shrine to the goat-god Pan.

It was there that Simon declared Jesus to be the Messiah. And it was there that Jesus gave Simon the name Peter or Cephas.[149] Now usually Peter is translated *rock* but that is missing so much of the richness of its Aramaic equivalent. Cephas is basically *cornerstone* and refers to the very first building block of a house—in this case, the very first building block of the church. Cephas is related to 'kippur', the name of the day. It is also a reference to the mercy seat covering the Ark of the Covenant. The mercy seat was the place the high priest would atone for the sins of the nation through the sprinkling of sacrificial blood—just once a year, on this special day, Yom Kippur.

Now when Jesus spoke to Simon and instituted the church, a moment of conception occurred. There's a birth in process that would culminate nearly nine months later at Pentecost—widely described as the 'birthday of the church'. But there's also a building in process: the cornerstone has just been laid.

Six days later, in the Cloud, the moment of implantation occurred when God confirmed His Son's identity. If, in the natural world in a woman's womb, implantation of a fertilised egg does not occur by this point, then the pregnancy will not proceed. So, as hinted by the timing here, as well as the words of God which, according to Dwight Pryor,[150] are those of a midwife, we can see the significance of the event for the unborn church.

All this occurred during Sukkot. This festival specifically commemorates God's Cloud of glory. During Sukkot, rough shelters are made overlaid with palm branches or leafy boughs. The sky must be visible while inside the booth, so the leaves must be placed in a trellis-like arrangement. The flimsy covering is a symbolic reminder of the thin covering of the Cloud that was an overshadowing and a protection during forty years of wilderness wandering. We are to be reminded that it's not the density of the Cloud that is our security but the God who descends in the Cloud.

The 'Cloud' of Sukkot is a thin open weave covering on the roof. And this is what Lilith's net counterfeits. It's a thin open weave snare, designed not to protect but to entrap. The overshadowing of the Holy Spirit is there for our protection. It was there for the protection of Jesus while He was in Mary's womb. It was there for the protection of the church in the interval between Yom Kippur and Pentecost. It will be there for us as we are in the process of giving birth to our own calling. But we can't let the moment of implantation of that calling pass—we have to head up the mountain with Jesus. And I mean 'up the mountain' in the metaphorical sense rather than the literal. I mean it in the sense of facing our fears, as Elijah finally did, when he met with Jesus in the place he was most afraid to go. I mean it in the sense of marching with Jesus into the war council where Anat and her allies are assembled and announcing that their rule in the Jerusalem of our lives is at an end. We have a new Cornerstone, just as was promised. He will make our covenants with them null and void— He has already paid the price to atone for our sins, to ransom us from Sheol and from Death and to cut off all agreements that would give them legal rights to retain our inheritance and to drain us of resurrection life. In addition, He makes us a remarkable promise:

'I tell you the truth, if you had faith even as small as a mustard seed, you could say to this mountain, "Move from here to there," and it would move. Nothing would be impossible.'

Matthew 17:20 NLT

'This mountain,' said Jesus. This statement occurred when He had returned to Caesarea Phillipi after the Transfiguration. I believe He wasn't so much referring to the physical height of Mount Hermon as what it signified: it was the power base of the principalities of this world, as well as authorities and world-rulers, just as it had once been the portal for the descent of the Watchers. That's what I think Jesus meant: all we need is a *little* faith and none of those great spiritual powers can stand against us.

But that little and insignificant faith needs to be joined to the faith of Jesus to be effective. That's the key.

Anat wants to defile both the Cornerstone and the Cloud so that we use our own faith, trying to rachet it up so it will be sufficient in God's eyes so we get the big tick that ushers us into our calling. But it's never about *our* faith. Ours could reach from here to the other side of the universe and it wouldn't be enough. Only the faith of Jesus our mediator is sufficient. That's why we have to place our mustard seed in His hand so He can wield it on our behalf.

The Cornerstone and the Cloud are not the only coverings Anat wants to despoil. She'd really like to confiscate our mantles—those gifts that have come down the family of faith from past generations. These are the legacies that Jesus has gifted into our hands, not so that we can repeat the works of those who went before us but so that we can advance their incomplete assignments towards the finish.

As I've mentioned previously, I realised the significance of Anat when looking at Hebrew word-lists for *time* while I was researching John's gospel. I'm not going to go into detail justifying what I'm about to say; that's done elsewhere.[151] I'm just going to summarise my findings in this conclusion.

When I was examining the first and last chapters, I was surprised to discover the wealth of clues about inheritance hidden in the text—and absolutely astounded when I realised John had indicated that Jesus had passed on Elijah's mantle to Simon Peter! His task was to finish Elijah's assignment of bringing a knowledge of Yahweh to the Gentiles.[152]

And then when I was researching the second and second-last chapters my astonishment, great as it was, went up several notches as I realised John had indicated Jesus passed Joseph's mantle to Mary Magdalene! He'd tasked her with continuing the work of undoing the dispossession Joseph had inaugurated.

And then in the third and third-last chapter, Nicodemus was given the mantle of Moses! Nicodemus, by the way, was a nickname. He was incredibly famous in the first century—he was regarded as only the third person in all of history who'd prayed to God and was answered with a time-altering miracle. Yes, Nicodemus understood the summoning of *appointed time*.

Moving further on into the fourth chapter, a woman of Samaria is appointed as the cupbearer of Jesus and given the mantle of the cupbearer Nehemiah.

A mantle is not about repeating the works of those who have worn it in the past. Rather, it's about taking on the legacy of our forebears in the faith and, with the help of our two Paracletes—Jesus and the Holy Spirit—advancing the unfinished parts of their assignment towards completion. It's also about recapitulation—that work of Jesus in binding up and mending the wounds of the past. It's about the healing of history and of time—we are called to exercise the ministry of recapitulation, just as Jesus was. We are called to step into stories that parallel past tragedies and change the endings.

Jesus at Cana said, *'My time is not yet come,'* but then He summoned the future to Himself and reset the appointed time, so that it entered the present. But He also summoned the past—He reached out to Joseph's decision to disinherit the Egyptians and He overturned it in a symbolic act of returning inheritance and birthright—creating new wine.

Yes, a miracle on that scale might test our faith to breaking capacity. But it surely does not test our faith to ask for a cup of water, as Jesus did at Sychar, thereby overturning Nehemiah's exile of foreign women. And it surely does not test our faith to accept an invitation to dinner, as Jesus did at Emmaus, thereby overturning the events of an ancient civil war that pitted one of the tribes of Israel against all the others.

For some believers the simplicity of these actions is an encouragement; for some, they are a discouragement. Some of us desire the spotlight and these actions are too ordinary for that. We feel the need to be acclaimed as heroes, rather than simply acknowledge that God has used us—*even us*—as 'instruments of the good'.[153]

We might ask ourselves why, of all people, Mary Magdalene was chosen by Jesus to inherit the mantle of Joseph. Along the ages it had passed through the many hands—but only a few were able to advance the legacy and not lose it. Sheerah, Joshua and Deborah were among those few. I think the reason Jesus gave it to the Magdalene was because the mantle was tainted by Anat. Any attempt to attack Mary with shame would not succeed because she was so far beyond it. Dispossession could no longer affect her: she would never lose the ultimate inheritance, Jesus Himself. She could therefore be entrusted with a mantle where there was an unfinished task of overturning dispossession and opposing Anat.

He chooses the weak and humble to confound the wise and mighty. Many of His actions were so simple, yet so deeply, wondrously profound.

In the end, it's all about Jesus. It always was and ever will be.

Prayer

Heavenly Father,

I ask to be secured under Your overshadowing 'wings'—Your prayer shawl—and protected by Your holy angels.

I renounce the counterfeit gifts of wisdom, understanding, knowledge, counsel, and might that the spirit of dispossession has given my family across many generations. I renounce too the counterfeit gifts of light and protection, security at night and in war, refuge for my children and grandchildren, appointment into a position of authority that was not meant for me or for us, agreement with the dispossession of a position of authority that was actually meant for me, appointment at the wrong time, hope restored out of season so that disillusionment would be complete. I ask Jesus as my mediator and the Holy Spirit as my advocate to empower my words of renunciation, waking them to life and giving them the drive to complete the work You have assigned to those words.

I ask instead to be one with Jesus as my covenant defender and to know His wisdom, understanding, knowledge, counsel, might and fear of the Lord. He has already won full restoration of inheritance for me and I ask Him to summon the time of its appearing into my lifetime, so that I can fulfil the calling and the destiny He has laid out for me and for my family. I thank Him for the mantle He wants to hand to me—and I ask Him to cleanse it seven times over and to help me to wear it to bring honour and glory to His name.

I thank Him for the promise of this amazing gift and restoration. I don't know what my inheritance will look like when it's returned, because I'm not even sure how many centuries it's been lost. But I look forward to seeing the bud, the flower and the fragrant fruit as it blooms and ripens in my life.

Thank You, Father.

Thank You, Jesus of Nazareth.

Thank You, Holy Spirit.

Thank You, blessed Trinity.

Amen and amen.

Live a life worthy
of the *calling* you have received.
Be completely *humble* and *gentle*;
be patient, bearing with one another in love.
Make every effort
to keep the unity of the Spirit
through the bond of peace.
There is *one body* and *one Spirit*,
just as you were called to one hope
when you were called;
one Lord, one faith, one baptism;
one God and Father of all,
who is *over all* and *through all*
and *in all*.

Ephesians 4:1–6 NIV

Appendix 1

Summary of Lilith's Tactics

(1) Through trauma, we will be **fixed to a spot** in the past. Emotionally, we will feel we are staked, stabbed, pinned, speared, transfixed. We will be drained through the wound.

(2) If we are freed from the fixed spot, **spiritual 'harpoons'** may be launched to slow us down or a **lasso** may be thrown to pull us back and corral us. We will be drained through the wound.

(3) A **'net' is used to entangle us**; this can be deployed at any point and is a counterfeit of the overshadowing protective Cloud of God's glory.

(4) **Blockage of the processing of shame**, leading to narcissism or to addiction. Shame binds itself to other emotions, including fear—thus helping create the 'net' of toxic beliefs knotted together.

(5) **Provocation of destructive behaviour** that we simply can't stop—addictions of all kinds, including the addiction to the toxic enabling of others so their processing of shame is blocked; self-sabotage including impatience that results in an inability to wait for the most appropriate moment to act or speak. An addiction to haste—a craving for the appointed time to be *now*; a compulsion to not 'let go'. All these result from inability to trust God.

(6) **The truce** that is conditional on not involving Jesus. We are willing to agree to this because we don't really trust Him. Sometimes we have just enough Jesus in our lives to not alert us to anything wrong. We are therefore lulled into complacency that we can live life without Jesus. We can even process shame without any covering from Jesus by reclassifying sin so that adultery becomes love, narcissism becomes self-care, abuse becomes pre-emptive self-defence, theft becomes restoration, pride becomes self-esteem.

(7) **Promise of safety.** An alliance, bargain or deal with Lilith is a temptation to security via a permanent truce. 'If you won't interfere with me, I will stay away from you.' God does not promise us safety in these terms: He promises us refuge in trouble and defence in battle. But

He does not promise that there will be no war. He grants us peace in the midst of strife, not a truce. The price of safety is often silence—a bargain to agree not to expose Lilith.

(8) **Manufacture of consent**—we don't have to say 'yes' to an agreement with Lilith, Anat, Sheol or Death. We have accepted their deal by simply not saying no. Silence is regarded as assent.

(9) **Removal of fence or boundary.** If a spiritual 'fence' is removed, then allegedly there's no transgression of boundaries, but an increase in creativity because of the greater area to play in. Belial and Lilith work in alliance here: Belial wants you to transgress boundaries deliberately; Lilith aids you in transgressing them by taking down the boundaries so you don't know they are there. Her lie is: if you don't know the law, you can't break the law. God however says that ignorance is no excuse, for the law is written in our hearts. This allows us to be dispossessed not just of 'territory' but of whatever we have built on that 'territory'—like a house built over a boundary onto the wrong block of land.

(10) In her aspect as a siren, Lilith **disrupts communication** with God and also sends out signals to commence violence.

(11) **The truth is weaponised to counteract meekness**, the Fruit of the Spirit, given to us as a specific weapon against Anat. God's Word is also weaponised, often through the projection of shame that we have insufficient faith. Honour can also be weaponised as a control mechanism, particularly in honour-shame cultures.

(12) Anat will attempt to confiscate or **steal the mantle** Jesus has prepared to hand to us, or perhaps tear it in half. The taking of the mantle **pushes out the appointed time** for the fulfilment of our calling beyond our lifetime.

(13) Encouraging us to accept and/or maintain a **covenant with Death** and an **agreement with Sheol** in combination with a **false refuge**.

(14) **Counterfeiting** spiritual light, wisdom, understanding, counsel, knowledge, might and encouraging us to fear her more than the Lord.

(15) Causing our **prayers** to be **answered in reverse** because Egyptian spiritualism has a hold on our lives.

Appendix 2

Summary

LILITH HAS A MULTIPLICITY of guises that include the well-known Greek goddess Athena, the obscure Canaanite goddess Anat and other identities such as Neith, Hebat, Hannahannah, Inanna, Ishtar and Minerva. Her symbols include taloned creatures such as owls and lions, as well as piercing things such as thorns, barbs, spears, javelins, lances, harpoons, spikes, arrows, needles, jabs and stabs. As Neith and Hannahannah, she is also associated with the bee and its sting. She is vampiric in nature. The word, Lilith, is related to *night* and was used a few centuries before Christ to describe the wives of the Watchers, those fallen angels who descended to earth to mate with beautiful human women. These wives were otherwise designated as sirens.

As the spirit of dispossession, Lilith is intent on dominating men, crushing and feeding off women and killing children. Her particular targets are those with prophetic gifts.

Her name appears only once in Hebrew, in Isaiah 34:14, although she was mentioned several more times in the Greek translation of the second century before Christ. As Anat, however, she appears in several place names including Jeremiah's hometown of Anathoth, just outside Jerusalem. This may be the place known as Bethany in Jesus' time. Anat's name is also present in connection with the judge Shamgar ben Anath as well as Joseph's wife, Asenath. She may also be the 'Queen of Heaven' mentioned by Jeremiah. One of her titles, Anat of Zaphon, is present in the name Zaphenath-Paneah, given by Pharaoh to Joseph.

Anat is also associated, like Kairos, with appointed time, and with the notion that violent sacrifice is necessary to be able to successfully seize hold of a passing opportunity. She is able to delay the appointed time for our calling, pushing it out so far that it can occur well beyond our lifetime. She dispossesses us not simply of fullness of life, inheritance in Christ, but also time and calling. Anat, Lilith and Kairos are all imaged as winged deities. This is rare. Anat's violence is so extreme and anarchic that the conflict with her is a war for the soul of civilisation.

Lilith blocks the processing of shame, leading to hiding, covering up, blame-shifting, truth-spinning by leaving out crucial details, and accusing the innocent. To process shame, it needs to be converted to guilt, so that the guilt can be dealt with through repentance. Lilith can use God's word as a weapon to shame us, instead of convict us. She also weaponises truth in a similar way, along with the giving of prophetic words 'out of season' so that hope withers and discouragement results.

Lilith's occult speciality is necromancy, that is, divination performed by consulting the shades of the dead. The agreement with Sheol, *the grave* or *the afterlife*, mentioned by Isaiah in combination with a covenant with Death is an exchange of sight for knowledge. A seer, a prophet with an ability to see into the spiritual realm, is involved in a trade for knowledge. Such occult insight, particularly if combined with healing, is a convincing testimony of spiritual power. However, unless it is accompanied by the Fruit of the Spirit—the only evidence Jesus judged as worthy—then there is no guarantee the power involved is of the Holy Spirit. The Fruit of the Spirit that is effective against Lilith is gentleness or meekness, *strength under control.*

Mankind is incredibly inventive when it comes to creating false refuges—places of consolation away from God. However, Anat is willing to help in this regard and her favourite ploy when it comes to false refuges is the 'truce'—with its mandatory condition, *Let's leave Jesus out of this.*

Very few of the major figures of faith in the Hebrew Scriptures contended with Anat and struggled to the point of actually overcoming her. Some were clearly terrified and abandoned their calling. Joseph, Moses, Samson, Saul, David, Elijah, Elisha, Jonah and Ahab did not escape her claws.

John's gospel lays out a trail of clues that suggest Jesus gave Mary Magdalene an identity as a direct counterpoint to Anat of Zaphon and bestowed on her Joseph's mantle with its unfinished business of returning inheritance. Then Jesus partnered with Mary in the total despoilation of Canaanite religion and liturgy, with a particular focus on the epic of Baal-Hadad and Anat. If Jesus wasn't able to work through this matter of dispossession without a woman by his side, and Barak wasn't able to do it without Deborah either, it's unwise to try to regain our inheritance without a similar male-female alliance. Even Joshua who, at first sight, appears to have overcome Anat alone needed the help of a woman—his long-dead kinswoman Sheerah who created the covenantal space he needed to have the victory over five armies.

Isaiah indicates that to bring the appointed time to pass when the Lord will annul a covenant with Death and an agreement with Sheol, we must:

- stop our mocking
- repent of our false refuges
- ask for and accept a new Foundation and Cornerstone
- stay with the Cloud, and
- refuse any threshing floor that is not of the Lord's wisdom.

We are to rely on Him also for knowledge, counsel, understanding, might. And we are to fear Him, not Anat.

With our new Cornerstone Jesus we are promised we will never be put to shame.

Endnotes

1 The degree to which we are motivated by fear is the degree to which we have accepted the mindset that we are lacking in provision and protection from God.

2 By physical state transitions, I mean such shifts as ice-to-water, liquid-to-gas, sub-sonic to super-sonic speeds through the sound barrier, kindling point or auto-ignition temperature.

3 Alternate names include 'Anat, Anath, Anaitis, Anait and Anat-bethel. She is also ironically called Rahmay or Rahmaya, *the Merciful*. This is also the title of one of the two wives of El, with Athirat-of-the-Sea, who are the mothers of the godlings of *Dawn* and *Dusk*, Shachar and Shalem. As Anatha-Baetyl or Anat-Bethel, likely of Syrian origin, she is sometimes called the wife of Yahweh. In Egypt she could be called Antit. Several etymologies of Anat's name have been proposed. A common view is it is a cognate of the Arabic word "anwat', *force* or *violence*. Anat could also mean *sign*. Her titles include Anat of Zaphon and her epithets are *Adolescent Anat* and 'Batalat 'Anat', *the Maiden, Sister of the Mighty One* (Ba'al). See: deity-of-the-week.blogspot.com/2011/11/anat.html (accessed 10 Ocotber 2022)

4 Besides *owl*, some translations render 'lilith' as *nighthawk*. Lilith, like Ziz, the spirit of forgetting, can be imaged as a taloned bird.

5 See Leviticus 17:7, 2 Chronicles 11:15 and Isaiah 13:21. Fourteen other references to the goat chosen to be the scapegoat may also fit into this category, since

that goat is sent to Azazel, an angelic prince imaged as a goat-demon. It is difficult for many scholars to believe that Azazel is, in fact, a goat-demon to whom God would command an offering to be sent each year on the Day of Atonement. However, in the light of Jesus' action on the Day of Atonement in the year before He died—going to Caesarea Philippi to the shrine of Pan, a half-human half-goat hybrid deity—I do not think it is tenable to consider Azazel as anything other than a demonic entity. See *Dealing with Azazel: Spirit of Rejection—Strategies for the Threshold #7*, Armour Books 2021

6   The Babylonian Talmud is a collection of Jewish writings compiled in the fifth century AD. It is the central teaching text of rabbinic Judaism. An earlier collection is called the Jerusalem Talmud.

7   This spelling is used by Rabbi Jonathan Sacks at rabbisacks.org/covenant-conversation/acharei-mot/the-scapegoat/ (accessed 12 January 2023)

8   These three steps are found in Henry Malone, *Shame: Identity Thief*, Vision Life Ministries International Inc 2006

9   Most emotions fade over time but shame can actually do the opposite. Also guilt, if left unremedied for a long period of time, can become shame. See: markmanson.net (accessed 3 July 2023) Language advisory: Manson uses lots of swearwords in an otherwise excellent article.

10 See, for example, Matthew 9:5.

11 John 8:11 NIV

12 John 8:11 BSB

13 'Shame is one of the big six negative emotions every child needs to lean to navigate by 18 months of age,

along with sadness, fear, anger, disgust and hopeless-despair.' Tom Hawkins, quoting Jim Wilder in Henry Malone, *Shame: Identity Thief*, Vision Life Ministries International Inc 2006

14   Hebrews 2:18

15   Brené Brown describes narcissism as the shame-based fear of being ordinary. See: *Daring Greatly: How the Courage to Be Vulnerable Transforms the Way We Live, Love, Parent, and Lead*, Avery 2012

16   Bruce Feiler, *Where God Was Born: A Journey by Land to the Roots of Religion*, William Morrow 2005

17   Anat, the spirit of appointed time, is allied with Kronos, the spirit of abuse and ordinary time. Anat's other persona Lilith, the vampiric spirit of dispossession, naturally partners with Belial, the spirit of armies and abuse.

18   See: *Dealing with Python: Spirit of Constriction—Strategies for the Threshold #1*, Armour Books 2017

19   2 Corinthians 6:15 NIV

20   Lilith is sometimes depicted standing on two lions. See: Henry O. Thompson, *Mekal, the god of Beth-Shan*, EJ Brill 1970

21   For more about Joseph and Pharaoh Aperanat, see *Name Covenant: Invitation to Friendship—Strategies for the Threshold #3*, Armour Books 2018

22   To confirm he meant these parallel quotes as genuine allusions to Joseph of Egypt, John mentions Joseph of Arimathea. And in addition there's the ultimate strangeness of Jesus making the dream of Pharaoh's cupbearer come *literally* true. In that dream, three branches on a vine budded, blossomed and burst into clusters. The cupbearer took the grapes, squeezed the juice into a cup and handed it to his master. All in a single fluid action. So similar to the miracle of Jesus. The astonishing transformation of water into wine is primarily about time, not about any unnatural chemical reaction. Water normally changes into wine over a long period of time in a grape vine. Jesus simply turned months into minutes—that's the real miracle. And to complete the parallel, both the wedding feast and Pharaoh's birthday, when Joseph's prophesied the cupbearer would return to his office, happened on 'the third day'.

23 See: rabbisacks.org/covenant-conversation/mikketz/joseph-and-the-risks-of-power/ (accessed 21 June 2023)

24 Again, however, Joseph uses the ambiguous term 'elohim' for *God* in Genesis 50:20.

25 1 Chronicles 7:21

26 It seems Sheerah took after her grandfather who also built cities. Joseph's were storehouse-towns for grain, but we don't know Sheerah's motivation.

27 This is particularly so since Sheerah's grandmother, Asenath, was not only named after Anat but may have had considerable religious input into the lives of her children and grandchildren.

28 The only other person in Scripture who has Sheerah, *remnant*, as part of his name is Isaiah's son, Sheer-Jashub.

29 The cities of Beth-Horon were, chronologically, the very last places mentioned in the historical portion of the Hebrew Scriptures. Nehemiah is the last Hebrew book if they are placed in order of time period. He finishes his account with a brief mention of an opponent from Beth-Horon. All this is a testimony to Sheerah's foresight. In taking up this inheritance, she

30 would have been in automatic opposition to Anat, the dispossessor.

30 Not least because the time span between Aperanat as the Pharaoh of Joseph's era and Rameses as the Pharaoh of the Exodus fits the biblical timeline.

31 When it says in Exodus 4:19 ESV, *'Go back to Egypt, for all the men who were seeking your life are dead,'* I have to make the assumption that *'all the men'* does not include Rameses himself. Therefore, I believe that, although Exodus 2:15 says Pharaoh sought to kill Moses, it is no longer his intention forty years later. Those who would still demand Moses' death are, as Exodus 4:19 mentions, now deceased.

32 Horemheb first rose to prominence as an army commander under Tutankhamen.

33 The vizier's name was Paramesse. When Paramesse became Pharaoh, he assumed the throne-name Rameses.

34 The one fly in the ointment of this reconstruction of identities is that Bint-Anat's tomb/sarcophagus has been discovered. We can however easily pluck the fly out—because the body in the tomb is male, not female.

35 David too in the 8th year of his reign conquered Jerusalem and moved there. This was almost half a millennium after Joshua's conquest. It wasn't worth prioritising by Joshua or any of the Judges.

36 thetorah.com/article/the-tabernacle-in-its-ancient-near-eastern-context (accessed 5 January 2024)

37 Commentators describe them as falcons, but they still have a cherubim-like look to them. Moreover, cherubim are found depicted in many cultures, always guarding thrones or sacred trees. See: hermeneutics.

	stackexchange.com/questions/77811/cherub-two-or-four-wings-how-did-ezekiel-know-they-were-cherubim (accessed 6 March 2024)
38	On the other hand, perhaps Ishtar is not the best example, since she is sometimes considered to be equivalent to Anat.
39	This is not an unusual action on God's part. Jesus does not come for millennia after the promise to Adam and Eve that a saviour will come; in the meantime, the Watcher angels tried to pre-empt and disrupt God's salvation of humanity by introducing their own nature into the children of the women they chose as mates.
40	Exodus 33:11
41	Moses in the triumphal Song of the Sea (Exodus 15) even appropriates the language of the poem celebrating Rameses' victory at Kadesh. See: theoutwardquest.wordpress.com/2015/03/11/berman-the-song-of-moses-and-ramses-iis-inscriptions/ (accessed 13 January 2024)
42	See: en.wikipedia.org/wiki/Amarna_letter_EA_287 (accessed 13 January 2024)
43	1 Kings 11:36 NIV
44	1 Kings 9:3 NIV
45	One meaning of Jericho is *fragrance*, relating to nose; Ai means both *city* and *eye*; Hazor is related to *sound* and thus to the ear and hearing.
46	Judges 17:6 NKJV
47	The existence of these guilds has been attested by numerous arrowheads dated from the 11th century before Christ found near Bethlehem between

1954 and 1980 at Solomon's Pools. These bronze arrowheads were inscribed in a formulaic way: [name] son of [deity]. One of these, now in the Israel Museum, has the engraving, 'Abdlabit, son of Anat.' See: imj.org.il/en/collections/375296-0 (accessed 14 January 2024)

48 Neith, the Egyptian equivalent of Anat had an annual light-lamp-torch festival that was said to be celebrated throughout the whole country. Athena, likewise, was associated with lamps and lights. Other goddesses linked with lights, light-bearing, light-bringing and lamp-lighting were Minerva, Astarte, Asthoreth, Isis and Ishtar.

49 See: herald-magazine.com/2021/01/01/deborah-and-jael-prevail-over-three-canaanite-goddesses/ (accessed 1 September 2023) This excellent article, *Deborah and Jael Prevail Over Three Canaanite Goddesses*, provides considerable detail on other goddesses, besides Anat, that were overcome in this battle.

50 Besides Anat, there was also Astarte, 'Mistress of Horse and Chariot', who was summoned in curses to smash the skulls of various enemies. Ironically, Sisera almost certainly worshipped Astarte but had his skull smashed by a woman. See: herald-magazine.com/2021/01/01/deborah-and-jael-prevail-over-three-canaanite-goddesses/ (accessed 1 September 2023)

51 The names Anat (or Anath), Neith, Athena (the Greek equivalent of Anat) are all related. Perhaps there is also a relation between Anat and names like Nathan, Nathanael and Jonathan. Nathan means *to give, to put, to set, to fix, to appoint.* Perhaps the notion of *appointed* in respect to *time* derives from a combination of 'nat' and 'eth' in the name Anat. The use of the name Nathanael instead of Bartholomew in

the first chapter of John's gospel might therefore be an initial pointer towards Anat's hidden presence in the second chapter.

52 Peter C. Craigie argued that the stars are part of Anat's retinue. See: Mark Smith and Wayne Pitard, *The Ugaritic Baal Cycle, Volume II. Introduction with Text, Translation and Commentary of KTU/CAT 1.3-1.4*, Vetus Testamentum, Supplements, Volume 114, Brill 2009

53 His breaches of the Nazarite vow included his touching of the dead—a lion he'd killed (Judges 14:8-9), thirty men whose clothes he stripped from their dead bodies (Judges 14:19), in the midst of a thousand dead men (Judges 15:14-16) who were killed using the jawbone of a dead donkey (Judges 15:15-17). It also likely included the drinking of wine at his wedding to the unnamed Philistine woman.

54 People who are narcissistic constantly use blame-shifting and projection to avoid processing their shame.

55 Oddly, he took his father and mother and put them under the protection of the king of Moab. However, he did not seek refuge in Moab himself.

56 David's choice in seeking refuge with the Philistines is a curious one. Certainly he could not have gone to Edom, as Saul obviously had an alliance there. However, he could have gone to Geshur since at one point he married a princess from there. She was the mother of Absalom. He could have gone to Ammon or Egypt or Amalek or Aram or the Jebusites. Or even Moab where he'd sent his parents. Yet, instead of doing any of these, he created a double-bind by going to the Philistines. In later years David doesn't ask God if He wants a Temple, but when his family are captured he asks God if he should rescue them.

Because of the double-bind, whatever David did at that point was going to be wrong. Asking God was a way of avoiding blame.

57 See: Anne Hamilton, *Where His Feet Pass: Jesus and the Healing of History 04*, Armour Books 2021

58 Ish-bosheth means *man of shame* and that, of course, is not what Saul named his son. He was Esh-Baal, *man of Baal*. In the early days of the kingship, this was probably not associated with the spirits but with God as *master* and *lord*. Ish-bosheth seems to be the chronicler's reframing of the name to project shame. Saul himself was a man pursued by shame. He came from Gibeah, the town where one of the most shameful acts in Israelite history had occurred, an act that provoked a civil war and the almost complete destruction of the tribe of Benjamin. The shame was intense throughout his life. He also tries to transfer shame to Jonathan in the incident involving David in 1 Samuel 20.

59 It's difficult to be sure that it was; it may have been Geba or Gibeah or Gibeath.

60 4.4 miles or 7 km.

61 Michael Heiser considers that 'elohim' means *resident of heaven* and therefore refers to God or to angels. I make the case in *Dealing with Kronos* that 'elohim' is ambiguous, but that 'ha'elohim' is not and that it refers only to angels. This influences how we interpret, for example, the request to Abraham to sacrifice Isaac which came from 'ha'elohim'.

62 It also had the advantage that it was *not* Gibeah. That town, since the time of the Judges, had an unsavoury reputation and, even many hundreds of years later, was still associated in the minds of the Jewish people with corruption and depravity. *'The things My people* *do are as depraved as what they did in Gibeah long ago.'* (Hosea 9:9 NLT)

63 2 Samuel 2:14

64 Disappointment involves a time factor for some people; they did not receive what they wanted or expected at the desired time. For other people, the disappointment revolves around value—they might receive what they wanted but the value is not commensurate with what they anticipated.

65 Arthur Burk uses the term 'Egyptian heresy' but that term can refer to both heretical Christian dogma and worship of Egyptian deities, as in New Age or Freemasonry. I have therefore used the term 'Egyptian spiritualism'.

66 See: Anne Hamilton, *Dealing with Resheph: Spirit of Trouble—Strategies for the Threshold #6*, Armour Books 2020

67 His true name was apparently Merib-baal. Once again, a nickname encoded with shame was given to him. Whether this was in his own lifetime or a retrospective dubbing by the chroniclers is unknown. He had an uncle, allegedly also called Mephibosheth, who was one of the men sacrificed by the Gibeonites.

68 2 Samuel 21:9 NIV

69 Jesus re-enacts or recapitulates the Fall so as to correct the erroneous actions of Adam. See: tmc.org.au (accessed 7 February 2024)

70 David didn't just sacrifice the sons of Saul. He also sacrificed the young men who were besieging Rabbah of the Ammonites in order to cover up Uriah's murder. In addition he may also have sacrificed the people of Rabbah when the city was eventually taken. There is some ambiguity in the text about his actions. However, the Septuagint—the Greek translation of the Hebrew, completed a few centuries before Christ— translates the passage to indicate he tortured and killed the inhabitants. When it comes right down to it, Joab and David have two things in common. The first: they are both have an immensely callous streak. And the second: they are both intensely loyal to the same person—David himself.

71 At this time Ahab was sending out messengers to neighbouring countries with veiled threats, in case they were harbouring Elijah. God's direction to Elijah to go to Zarephath near Sidon was both cunning and compassionate—the city was in the territory of Ahab's father-in-law. It's the last place anyone would suspect Elijah would go. And, even if he was found there, Ahab would not war against his wife's father.

72 They appear in the narrative of 1 Kings 20:13–43

73 The river Litani is named for Lotan, the seven-headed coiling monster that is the Canaanite equivalent of Leviathan.

74 It is termed a master emotion because it can internalise many other negative emotions. See: Henry Malone, *Shame: Identity Thief*, Vision Life Ministries International Inc 2006

75 Jehu was stationed at Ramoth-Gilead on the eastern side of the Jordan; Hazael was in Damascus further north; and Elisha was at Abel-Meholah, near Tishbe, Elijah's own hometown. Both Ramoth-Gilead and Abel-Meholah were in Gilead. All this meant that Elijah would not have to cross the Jordan to face Jezebel but could stay on the sunrise side to complete his assignment.

76 I could well be wrong but it seems to me that the fullness of the Gentiles coming into the Kingdom

reverses the fullness of the iniquity of the Amorites and thus their dispossession.

77 Elijah had met up with Jehu. We do not learn this until Jehu has just been anointed and is furiously driving to Jezreel. Having just killed Joram, Ahab's son, *'Jehu said to Bidkar, his chariot officer, "Pick him up and throw him on the field that belonged to Naboth the Jezreelite. Remember how you and I were riding together in chariots behind Ahab his father when the Lord spoke this prophecy against him.'* (2 Kings 9:25 NIV) Jehu then repeats the prophecy, thereby indicating he was a first-hand witness to Elijah's rebuke of Ahab. Consequently, it's clear Elijah met up with Jehu.

78 He threw his mantle over him which may perhaps be equivalent to an anointing.

79 The Canaanite equivalent of Leviathan.

80 Anat went to war against personified Fire and Flame. They were conceived of as dogs. See: Henry O. Thompson, *Mekal, the god of Beth-Shan*, EJ Brill 1970

81 See: Rev. Prof. John Gray M.A., B.D., Ph.D., *Legacy of Canaan: The Ras Shamra texts and their relevance to the Old Testament*, Series: Vetus Testamentum, Supplements, Volume 5, Brill 1965

82 *Sirens* are mentioned in the Septuagint in six verses, including three times in Isaiah (13:21, 34:13, 43:20), yet English translations of the Hebrew generally use *jackals* or *wild goats*. The Syriac *Apocalypse of Baruch* (*II Baruch*) provides strong evidence for Papoutsakis' reconstruction of Isaiah 13:21 as 'I will summon the sirens from the sea; and you, liliths, come from the desert, and (you), demons and jackals, from the forests.' See: hermeneutics.stackexchange.com/questions/19716/how-did-sirens-arise-in-the-septuagint-translation-of-isaiah-1321 (accessed 1 February 2024)

83 False refuges are detailed in *Hidden in the Cleft: True and False Refuge—Strategies for the Threshold #4*, Armour Books 2019

84 According to the ancient Greek poet Hesiod, fate is the daughter of night. This is another way of saying that appointed time, destiny and opportunity come from Lilith.

85 The first mention of a deity named Bethel outside of the Bible is in a treaty imposed on Baal I of Tyre by the Assyrian king Esarhaddon. Among other deities whose names are invoked in curses against Baal I—presumably if he should violate the terms of the treaty—we find the following: 'May Bethel and Anath-Bethel [deliver] you into the paws of a man-eating lion.'

86 He uses unusual words, words found nowhere else in Scripture. So perhaps he invented them, like the Shakespeare of his age, to evoke just the right nuance: he uses 'peliyliyyah' for the rendering of judgment in verse 7. The word suggests 'liyliyith', *owl* or Lilith.

87 Perhaps in Isaiah 28:20, the two references to *narrow*, 'sar', might refer to the infamously narrow path up to Sheerah's city as well as be puns on her name.

88 See: https://www.theopedia.com/recapitulation-theory-of-atonement (accessed 27 January 2024)

89 He also commented on the faithfulness of Mary compared to the faithlessness of Eve.

90 See for an explanation of these theories: faithrethink.com/7-atonement-theories-from-church-history/ (accessed 30 December 2023)

91 Some translations of Genesis 37:15 say, *'What are you looking for?'* but the Hebrew word for *what* can also be *who*. The Greek word for *who* in John 20:15 can also be *what*.

92 During Sukkot a total of 70 bulls were sacrificed during the festival. In the Baal epic, Anat slaughters 70 oxen, sheep, deer, goats and asses. She's always got to prove herself better than Yahweh, better than Jesus.

93 Adam J Howell, *The Neighbors of Bronze Age Israel: A Descriptive Study of Canaanite Religion*, academia.edu/16504061/The_Neighbors_of_Bronze_Age_Israel_A_Descriptive_Study_of_Canaanite_Religion (accessed 30 November 2022)

94 Ra'shu Yeni, the New Wine Festival, was held in the twelfth month of the Canaanite year, while Sukkot, the Feast of Tabernacles, was in the first month of the Jewish civic year. Nevertheless they were both celebrated at a similar time.

95 Luke does say *'about eight days'*. (Luke 9:28)

96 On the one hand, the ambition of the power behind the king of Babylon appears to come from Baal-Hadad the Cloud-Rider by the reference to 'the tops of the clouds' but on the other it seems to be Bull El, by the reference to 'Most High'.

97 As a general rule, this is undoubtedly true. But there are notable exceptions, as we already seen. Some Biblical chroniclers most definitely tried to project shame onto some people by recording the nicknames that encoded shame and thus attached it to their identity. This was particularly noticeable when it came to renaming the sons in the family of Saul and substituting 'bosheth', *shame*, for 'baal', *lord, master* or *husband*. Merib-baal was renamed Mephibosheth, Ishbaal was renamed Ishbosheth.

98 rabbisacks.org/ceremony-celebration-family-edition/yom-kippur-family-edition/ (accessed 1 March 2024)

99	rabbisacks.org/archive/without-shared-moral-code-can-freedom-society/ (accessed 1 March 2024)
100	Ugaritic poetry venerates Anat as 'Mistress of Kingship, Mistress of Dominion, and Mistress of the High Heavens.' encyclopedia.com/environment/encyclopedias-almanacs-transcripts-and-maps/anat (accessed 11 October 2023)
101	Bethany, where Jesus so often stayed, may have been Jeremiah's hometown of Anathoth (Beit Anathoth, Beit Anatot), named for Anat.
102	To demonstrate the inter-relation of our modern word 'memory' with Mary and also watchtower (Samaria), I can do no better than quote from the *Online Dictionary of Etymology* which lists the oldest common language root (shown here in **bold**):

> memory (noun): mid-13th century, recollection (of someone or something); awareness, consciousness, also fame, renown, reputation, from Anglo-French 'memorie' (Old French 'memoire', 11th century, mind, memory, remembrance; memorial, record) and directly from Latin 'memoria', memory, remembrance, faculty of remembering, abstract noun from 'memor', mindful, remembering, from PIE [**proto-Indo-European language**] root ***(s)mer-** , to remember (Sanskrit 'smarati', remembers, Avestan 'mimara', mindful; Greek 'merimna', care, thought, 'mermeros', causing anxiety, mischievous, baneful; Serbo-Croatian 'mariti', to care for; Welsh 'marth', sadness, anxiety; Old Norse Mimir, name of the giant who guards the Well of Wisdom; Old English 'gemimor', known, 'murnan', mourn, remember sorrowfully; Dutch 'mijmeren', to ponder. Meaning faculty of remembering is late 14th century in English.

(etymonline.com/word/memory — accessed 26 December 2017)

103 Just as it was six days after Simon was renamed Peter that the Transfiguration occurred.

104 John 20:15 NIV

105 'Only when shame outweighs the pain in a circumstance are we willing to deal with the shame.' Jack Frost, as quoted in Henry Malone, *Shame: Identity Thief*, Vision Life Publications 2006

106 See: library.biblicalarchaeology.org/wp-content/uploads/2023/11/Warrior-Women-BAR-Winter-2023.pdf (accessed 1 February 2024)

107 John 20:17 BLB

108 bible.com/fr/reading-plans/4601-the-christian-jewish-roots/day/17 (accessed 20 February 2024)

109 Dr. Eli Lizorkin-Eyzenberg, *Hebrew Insights from Revelation*, Independent 2021

110 Matthew 14:22–32

111 See in addition to John 2:19–21 as quoted here, Hebrews 9:1–28, and Hebrews 10:1–18

112 1 Peter 2:6, based on Isaiah 28:16.
See also Ephesians 2:20

113 John 8:12, 9:5 (compare the lampstand Exodus 25:31–39, Leviticus 24:3, 4, Isaiah 53:11, Psalm 56:13).

114 John 6:35, 41, 48 (compare Exodus 25:23–30, Leviticus 24:8).

115 1 Timothy 2:5

116 John 10:7

117   For the water of life or living water, see John 4:13–14, and for the laver Exodus 30:17–21. See also 1 Corinthians 6:11.

118   See John 1:29, 1 Corinthians 5:7, 1 Peter 1:19 and Exodus 12:1–14.

119   See Hebrews 4:14–16, 7:23–28, 9:15 and 12:24

120   Arthur Burk refers to this as the 'Egyptian heresy'.

121   Joe Medina, as quoted in Henry Malone, *Shame: Identity Thief*, Vision Life Publications 2006

122   Judges 4:4–10

123   The riddle may in fact be an oblique reference to Anat. *Out of the eater something to eat:* the consummate 'eater' for the Canaanites, and the Philistines who worshipped the same deities, was Mot, *Death.* But Mot was one of the 'young lions' killed by Anat. He was therefore a 'dead lion', just like the animal Samson had killed. Mot is also described as 'strong', indeed texts use him as a point of comparison—as 'strong as Mot'. So 'eater' suggests Mot and 'strong' confirms it. The rest of the riddle hints at a reversal: something sweet to eat coming forth from the eater, Mot—pointing towards fruit or honey. In keeping with the 'dead lion' motif in relation to Mot, this would then connect to his killer, Anat, and to the prophetic dream of her father about reversal of death when the wadis would flow with honey. Anat was often depicted as standing on a lion, and her Egyptian counterpart Neith was associated with a bee. Therefore Samson's riddle may, in some way, proclaim his ascendancy over Anat—he killed the lion that was her pedestal-chariot-throne and robbed the bees that symbolised her right to bestow the kingship where she decided.

124 In the first century, binding demons was an occult practice in Greece and Rome which is perhaps why we have no record of it in the gospels.

125 Comparing jihad with a Biblical view of warfare, Qureshi quotes an unnamed friend who articulated Rule #1: 'If you want to follow the biblical model of attacking a land, the first thing you have to do is wait 400 years.' Nabeel Qureshi, *Answering Jihad: A Better Way Forward*, Zondervan 2016

126 See: Anne Hamilton, *Dealing with Leviathan: Spirit of Retaliation—Strategies for the Threshold #5*, Armour Books 2020

127 The threat to abusers is also present—they need to be reasonably sure that anyone who becomes suspicious of grooming activity or molestation will not report it. With regard to Belial and abuse: it's not enough to groom the child, it's also important as part of the process to pre-emptively discredit potential whistle-blowers. These are the people who will not dismiss suspicious actions because of allegedly fine character. Most importantly, there is a sub-set of these people who will not only become suspicious but will use their voice on behalf of the vulnerable and not remain silent. Not everyone who becomes suspicious has the courage to speak out and risk an attack on their own reputation in the process. Such a person is the only real threat to the long-term success of any grooming process and they must be sidelined continually in the hope that marginalisation will make them leave. They are to be left out of any information loop, their invitations to events are to be lost in the mail, their knowledge about those events and access to them is to be restricted, they are to be spoken of complainers and trouble-makers as well as rumour-spreaders and gossipers of the most malign and vicious kind. They are simply not to be believed. This character take-down of a potential opponent preferably has to happen well in advance. It is a safeguard against exposure by those who intend to abuse.

128 It should be noted that 'I am right' is not only a vow but a false refuge, a protective mechanism.

129 This poem as well as other literature was found in the early twentieth century in Ugarit in present-day Syria.

130 Bringing others with Him, similar to the raising of the ghost army in *The Epic of Aqhat*.

131 For more information on the Rephaim and the Valley of Travellers, see Derek Gilbert at skywatchtv.com/2021/12/21/saturn10/ and skywatchtv.com/2021/12/23/saturn11/ (accessed 5 March 2024)

132 The reasons for omitting these two sites seem obscure, and perhaps politically motivated. However it is also possible Shechem, Shiloh and Mizpah are basically the same place. See: Anne Hamilton, *The Inviolable Kingdom*, Armour Books 2025

133 See: ijs.org.au/synagogue-services/ (accessed 19 February 2024)

134 David's message in co-opting an existing threshing floor may well have been: 'My god is stronger than yours.' It is consistent with ancient practice of using existing sanctified spaces. See: Bruce Feiler, *Where God Was Born: A Journey by Land to the Roots of Religion*, William Morrow 2005

135 Joice Loch, in describing her experiences in Greece in the early twentieth century, noted: 'Every man slept on the ground by his own sheaves ready to start winnowing when the wind blew across the threshing floor.' Joice NanKivell Loch, *A Fringe of Blue: An Autobiography*, Murray 1968

136 See: thetorah.com/article/gilgal-yhwhs-footprints-in-the-land-of-israel (accessed 29 February 2024)

137 It was not always the case that there were nearby tiered slopes but it was true in the majority. See: lipkintours.com/index.php?dir=site&page=articles&op=item&cs=3121 (accessed 29 February 2024)

138 Isaiah 66:1–4

139 See: childrenshealthdefense.org/defender/anthony-fauci-bioweapons-research-covid-wuhan-cover-up/?utm_id=20231206 (accessed 1 March 2024)

140 Although I haven't mentioned *bats* in relation to Lilith, because there does not appear to be any ancient symbolism that connects them, there is nonetheless an obvious link through both vampires and night.

141 The circular movement has, as some people have testified, an aspect of hypnotic 'fascination'.

142 Originally found at wnd.com/2015/04/the-armenian-genocide-and-my-grandmothers-secret/ (accessed 2015) This link no longer works but the Wayback Machine may provide archival details. If you would like the full article (it is quite long), please contact me.

143 Janissary troops were the mainstay of the Ottoman Empire for five hundred years. Young Christian boys were taken from their parents, brainwashed into mindless loyalty to the Sultan and converted to Islam (often to the Sufi sect). They were then sent out against the Sultan's enemies who, of course, would sometimes be their own families and people. This is a classic example of the philosophy prevalent in the Muslim world: our enemies will resource the war against themselves. Similarly, ISIS terrorists took Yazidi boys for the same purposes and, at the end of the Second Word War, Andarte operatives in Greece seized and trained boys and girls they captured; burned villages and carried off small children. (Joice NanKivell Loch, *A Fringe of Blue: An Autobiography*, Murray 1968)

144 Zephaniah 3:17

145 Neith, Anat's Egyptian counterpart, is called 'ruler of arrows' and pictured with a bow and arrows or a harpoon. See: thecuriousegyptologist.com/2021/05/14/neith-the-great-mother-and-ruler-of-arrows/ (accessed 24 January 2024)

146 Athena was worshipped throughout Israel. A statue was found at Beit She'an, pottery depicting her from the second century BC was found at Bethsaida and coins from the third century BC were found in the Jerusalem area of Judea.

147 See: uir.unisa.ac.za/bitstream/handle/10500/7875/thesis_palmer_mj.pdf.pdf (accessed 21 January 2024)

148 See: Mark S. Smith and Wayne T. Pitard, *The Ugaritic Baal Cycle Volume II Introduction with Text, Translation and Commentary of KTU/CAT 1.3–1.4*, Supplements to Vetus Testamentum, volume 114, Brill 2009

149 Jesus' words, *'Away from Me, Satan,'* during His temptation and His similar words to Peter, *'Get behind Me, Satan'* occurred exactly three years apart (by Jewish calendar reckoning). They also occurred in the same vicinity on or near Mount Hermon. The first statement was made on the high mountain where all the kingdoms of the world were displayed—thus indicating Mount Hermon, the seat of all seventy principalities. The second was made at Caesarea Philippi in the foothills of Mount Hermon.

150 Dwight Pryor, *Jesus—The Fullness of Tanakh*, in *Roots and Branches: Explorations in the Jewish Context of the Christian Faith*, John Fieldsend (ed.), Clifford Hill

(Editor), Walter Riggans (Editor), John C.P. Smith (Editor), Fred Wright (Editor), PVM Trust 1998. Pryor indicates God's language during the Transfiguration is that of a midwife. He also points out that, just a few days prior to this, Jesus had asked His disciples who people thought He was. God's answer to Jesus' question is not revealed until the Transfiguration and combines phrases from the Law (Moses), the Prophets (Isaiah) and the sacred writings (Psalms).

151 See Anne Hamilton, *The Summoning of Time: John 2 and 20—Mystery, Majesty and Mathematics in John's Gospel #2*, Armour Books 2024

152 See Anne Hamilton, *The Elijah Tapestry: John 1 and 21—Mystery, Majesty and Mathematics in John's Gospel #1*, Armour Books 2023.

153 I am indebted to Austin M. Freeman for this idea from *Tolkien Dogmatics: Theology through Mythology with the Maker of Middle-earth*, Lexham Press 2022. He points out that in JRR Tolkien's epic high fantasy novel, *The Lord of The Rings*, Frodo is tempted to despair through a last remnant of pride. He wishes to have returned as a hero, rather than as simply an *instrument of the good.* Condemning himself for his own failure, he will struggle against this reverse sort of pride for the rest of his life.

If you found this book helpful, other books in this series may prove useful too as you address the issues that bar your way into your calling:

Dealing with Python: Spirit of Constriction

Strategies for the Threshold #1

with Arpana Dev Sangamitrha

On the threshold into your unique calling in life a dark spiritual sentinel waits. Scripture names it 'Python'—it has a God-given right to be there and test your significant choices. Trying to cast it out of a situation is useless.

Paul encountered it just as the Gospel was transitioning across a major threshold: the watershed moment when Christianity moved from Asia to Europe.

This book explores the tactics of Python, as well as its agenda. It offers insight into what this spirit hopes to get out of you and how you can rectify past mistakes involving this constricting, cunning enemy.

Dealing with Ziz:
Spirit of Forgetting

Strategies for the Threshold #2

The most significant threshold point of life is the doorway into God's unique calling for us. He invites us through covenant to fulfil the destiny we were born to achieve.

However, many of us fall at the threshold, rather than pass over it. We experience constriction, wasting, retaliation and forgetting—to such a degree it's easy to doubt the promises of God.

Dealing with Ziz examines the spiritual implications of forgetting in relation to threshold covenants. Since the opposite of remembering is dismembering—dismembering of truth—the spirit of forgetting is able to block access to our calling.

Yet there is an answer, a Fruit of the Spirit that overcomes Ziz.

Name Covenant:
Invitation to Friendship

Strategies for the Threshold #3

Abram became Abraham. Jacob became Israel. Simon beame Peter.

Name covenanting seems at first like an archaic, long-discarded practice that disappeared in the first century around the time Saul became Paul. The patriarchs and apostles exchanged names and so received new destinies. But that was then. And this is now.

However name covenanting never went away.

Robert Louis Stevenson became Teriitera. Paul Gauguin became Tioka. James Cook became Terreeoboo. Arthur Phillip became Woollarwarre.

These recent examples throw light on this ancient practice of friendship and kinship. They show us that, when God offers a new name, more than simply a new calling is attached. It's an invitation to friendship with Him.

If you're wondering how to overcome the issues of the threshold and the associated ungodly covenants, this book has the answer. Other books help you recognise the problem, this one points out the first step on the path.

Hidden in the Cleft:
True and False Refuge

Strategies for the Threshold #4

Jesus had a refuge—a safe haven—He retreated to when His life was in danger.

What does His choice reveal about where best to find sanctuary in times of trouble? What is the significance of the hiding place He used for an entire season? How can we discern the difference between a true and false refuge?

Removal of our false refuges is the first step towards achieving our life's calling—the divine purpose for which God created us. Yet all too often we fail to recognise how we've defaulted to a false refuge when disappointment strikes.

This book offers practical help, hope and encouragement towards achieving your destiny in Christ.

Dealing with Leviathan:
Spirit of Retaliation

Strategies for the Threshold #5

Retaliation, reprisal, retribution—many of us express the ferocity of our encounters with the spirit of Leviathan with such words. Most believers are stunned by savagery of the backlash they experience, and are baffled by God's seeming failure to intervene.

Reparation, recompense, restitution, restoration—these promised corrections to injustice are smashed just as they seem within reach. Why does this happen?

As we examine Scripture, we find that Leviathan is an officer of God's royal court. When we violate the consecration of that Holy Place, it has the legal right to remove us. It does not do so gently.

Dealing with Leviathan offers insight into overcoming this spirit of the deep.

Dealing with Resheph:
Spirit of Trouble

Strategies for the Threshold #6

with Irenie Senior

Resheph is mentioned seven times in Scripture. A fallen seraph and throne guardian, it is identified here as a hidden face of Leviathan, the spirit that counterattacks against dishonour. Symbolised as a stag and an archer, Resheph is connected with flames and fire, fever, financial distress, mental illness, drought and scorching heat as well as the underworld.

Jesus warred against this spirit at least seven times. It's easy to miss these battles because it's easy to miss the prophecies Jesus was fulfilling and the mention of Resheph associated with them.

This is a companion volume to *Dealing With Leviathan* and examines the obstacles we face on the threshold into our calling.

Dealing with Azazel:
Spirit of Rejection

Strategies for the Threshold #7

'I am your only friend.'

That's the playbook line that works so superbly for the spirit of rejection. Most of us fall for it without ever realising our coping mechanisms—fight, flight, freeze, flatter, forestall or forget—are actually undermining our every effort to overcome this entity. So how can we subdue the spirit of rejection in our lives without sabotaging ourselves in the process?

This seventh book in the series, *Strategies for the Threshold*, addresses the nature of the spirit, its wider agenda, its spiritual legal rights, and its propensity for following after us to undo the good that we do.

Dealing with Belial:
Spirit of Armies and Abuse

Strategies for the Threshold #8

with Janice Speirs

'What harmony,' Paul asked, *'is there between Christ and Belial?'*

Where, you might wonder, did he pluck that name from? In most English Bibles, it appears for the first time in Paul's second letter to the Corinthians. So it comes as a surprise to realise this army commander of the spirit world is mentioned 27 times in Hebrew, almost always in connection with abuse and violence. Modern translations generally substitute *worthless.* Yet from the stories where Belial appears, we can draw important principles for dealing with its tactics, agenda and ploys.

This eighth book in the series, *Strategies for the Threshold*, examines the spiritual dynamics involved in approaching your life's calling.

Dealing with Kronos:
Spirit of Abuse and Time

Strategies for the Threshold #9

with Janice Speirs

The oldest stories about 'Father Time' describe an entity with a seraph's body, and heads like the angelic cherubim. Kronos is a voracious spirit of abuse who consumes the past. Bound in chains to prevent him eating the future, nevertheless through the power of unresolved past trauma he wants to devour the present too.

We can believe we've escaped abuse when, in reality, complicity with Kronos has locked us into a maximum security spiritual prison. We need the Redeemer of wasted time to aid us. Scripture provides unexpected and important principles for dealing with the tactics, agenda and ploys of Kronos.

This book is a companion volume to *Dealing with Belial*.

Core Values: Love

The DNA of God #1

with Rebekah Robinson

Taste and see that the Lord is good!

Galatians 5 describes the growing DNA of God in our lives as a list of attributes, or *fruit*, emanating from the Holy Spirit.

This first volume explores the love aspect of God's nature, and its outworking in the hearts of believers respective to His other flavours.

Core Values: Joy

The DNA of God #2

with Rebekah Robinson

The Kingdom of God is a matter of righteousness, peace, and joy in the Holy Spirit. This is a direct reflection of the nature of its King!

This second volume looks into the joy of the Lord, and how His joy overflows into our lives.

www.ingramcontent.com/pod-product-compliance
Lightning Source LLC
Chambersburg PA
CBHW030050100526
44591CB00008B/88